CUCUMBER
A
FISHNET TIGHTS

To Margaret & Billy
with my love
Margaret

March 6th 2006

CUCUMBER SANDWICHES AND FISHNET TIGHTS

MARGARET WALKER

To my dear husband, Michael

FAST TRACK PUBLISHING
WELWYN, ENGLAND

Cucumber Sandwiches and Fishnet Tights
Copyright © Margaret Walker 2006

ISBN 1-84426-355-X

First Published 2006 by
FAST TRACK PUBLISHING LTD
Welwyn, England.

Printed by Copytech UK Ltd.

Thanks to Michael, Christopher, Pauline and Rosie, who have shared with me the many ups and occasional downs of vicarage life, and especially to my men folk for proofreading.
Thanks also to all our parishioners, without whom there would have been no material for this book.
This book is based on true events, although in some instances fictitious names have been used.

Chapter 1

'I wish I'd married a dustman,' I muttered as I took out a battered tartan slipper from the greenery in the north aisle window, and prepared to do battle with the chief flower arranger, who was seething in the vestry after finding her prize gladioli neatly sliced into three inch pieces.

Over at the vicarage, my parents-in-law had just arrived. Michael's father was to be our Harvest preacher. They wanted coffee. Well, they could have it as long as they made it themselves and took charge of Miss Mandrick and her incriminating left slipper and pair of scissors, and didn't let her anywhere near the church for the rest of the morning. Poor lady – she was in the early stages of dementia, leading her to think that her left slipper would enhance the harvest decorations, and that gladioli stems looked best if snipped into short pieces.

Mrs Chief-Flower-Arranger did not agree.

'These gladioli cost me 75p each. What can I use to get my shape into this pedestal now? That woman shouldn't be allowed in church!'

Later that night I would think of a brilliant theological repartee to this statement, but it didn't do for the vicar's wife to get riled. In any case, by now my eyes had been drawn to a purple vision with walking stick, plodding inexorably towards the lectern, bearing two purple feather dusters.

I knew who it was immediately. We called her Mrs Purple Nixon and she was almost ninety. Her fiancé had been killed in the First World War, and her husband had died in the Second World War. She had no children. A fortune-teller had told her in 1946 that she should wear purple; it was her lucky colour. Thirty years later not only was she wearing purple, but she had a purple house, with purple chairs and purple cushions. The lectern, it seemed, was about to get the purple treatment too.

My husband, Michael, breezed in through the south door just as I was mentally betrothing myself to a dustman in my next life. Blissfully unaware of carpet slippers and three-inch gladioli stems, not to mention feather dusters, he put his arm round my waist and asked, 'Any chance of a cup of coffee?'

'Oh yes, there's a Mad Hatter's tea party on at the vicarage. Miss Mandrick's already there and you can take Mrs Purple Nixon with you!'

Mrs Flower-Arranger had been appeased by a five-pound note from the discretionary fund and had left in pursuit of second-best gladioli. Miss Mandrick and her scissors were to be kept at bay at all costs.

Michael returned with a flask of coffee. Perspective slowly reappeared. He helped me incorporate the two purple feather dusters into the lectern décor, making a nest for the purple grapes suspended on purple twine from the eagle's neck.

Already the apple-sweet fragrance of Harvest Festival was rising to the clerestory windows, and the font overflowed with a cornucopia of vegetables from the verger's garden. Deep purple Michaelmas daisies and bronze chrysanthemums, soon to be joined by uncut white gladioli, glowed from the sanctuary.

'All good gifts around us (slippers and feather dusters included)
Are sent from heaven above.
Then thank the Lord, O thank the Lord
For all his love.'

I wiped my green, stale chrysanthemum hands on my pinny and kissed my coffee-bearing husband. I really wouldn't want to be married to anyone else.

In fact, I had always wanted to be a vicar's wife. My mother had been a Sunday school superintendent and my father the church treasurer and churchwarden, so curates and vicars were regular visitors to our house. In my idealistic teens, I had held visions of myself in a large brimmed hat socialising with everyone on the vicarage lawn as I offered them thinly-cut cucumber sandwiches, then returning to wash up the china as my devout and holy husband, who never ever lost his temper, sat in the cosy glow of a pink table lamp in the study, preparing next Sunday's sermon.

But where to start? How do you find an eligible vicar?

Luck was on my side. Our old vicar had moved on and there were rumours that a new one had just been appointed. Could he be my man? The following Monday's *Hull Daily Mail* carried the story –"New Vicar for St. Mary's, Beverley". I read on, and saw the photo. He was 49, married, and bald. Obviously not for me. But wait! The last paragraph revealed that he had a son of 19 who was hoping to be ordained. Could he be my true romance?

Maybe we could have fallen for each other at first sight, but I hated his mustard-wool waistcoat and baggy khaki corduroy trousers. He, apparently, thought I had distinctly odd eyebrows. We were soon to part. He was off to Lampeter to do an arts degree, while I was off to read social administration at Nottingham University, where there were four boys to every girl. There was also a theology department. I joined the Anglican Society in whose meetings I could survey the field. Meanwhile, in deepest West Wales, the vicar's son was cocooned in an all-male community.

Two years and a few short romances later, the vicar's son and I were home for Christmas, and met up in the ringing chamber on practice night. Being tall and strong, he rang the tenor, while I took the treble bell.

'Treble's going, she's gone!' I called, as I pulled the bell off its stay to launch into rounds. My job was to keep my eyes on the tenor. Not a bad job; he was really quite handsome. He'd got rid of that silly side parting and I felt my fingers being lured to bounce on his curls. I'd never noticed what lush dark eyebrows and eyelashes he had, and how wonderfully they framed his cornflower blue eyes. Khaki cord trousers notwithstanding, I suddenly realised that treble was not only going but she was well and truly gone.

Six weeks later on a wet Saturday afternoon in my university 'digs', he proposed.

Two-and-a-half years later, the bells of St. Mary's, Beverley, rang out for our wedding. I left the reception in a large hat. The cucumber sandwiches would have to wait a while.

In the 1960s, ordinands had to ask their bishop for permission to marry. Michael was to serve in the York Diocese, so had to see the archbishop. Donald Coggan agreed that we could marry after Michael had served a reasonable stint as deacon. We interpreted this with some liberty and arranged the wedding for one month after his ordination in York Minster. Having it the last weekend in October had the unsought, but welcome advantage of giving us an hour extra in bed on our wedding night. Nine months later I gave birth to Christopher. Things were moving fast!

Chapter 2

'What does your husband do?'
'He's a priest.'

I wait for the comment this so often triggers, 'So, he only works one day a week!'

I can laugh it off now, but as a newlywed it made me angry. How could a seemingly intelligent person utter this statement, yet want his daughter's wedding on a Saturday, preceded by a rehearsal on Friday, expect the priest to visit his dying father on a Wednesday, make funeral arrangements on a Thursday, and forfeit his day off the following Tuesday to take the funeral service?

'Men in the Ministry', I soon learned, worked at best a six-day week, and their job was not a nine-to-five one. The day started with Morning Prayer in the parish church at 8am and finished after 10pm, when the youth club had disgorged from the decibel-filled church hall or the church council meeting had rambled to the concluding grace. Between these times were slotted in pastoral visiting, study, sermon-writing, hospital visits, administration, school assemblies, confirmation classes, bible-study groups and meetings with the other clergy.

St. Paul, in his letter to Timothy, exhorts a church leader, 'to be able to manage his own family well, for if a man does not know how to manage his own family, how can he take care of the Church of God?' With this I concurred, and felt that if the Church had allowed Michael to spend a bit more time with his wife and son, then his example to the flock would have benefited.

On the other hand, he was always popping in and out of the house, so I was never alone for long stretches of time, which was the fate of most of my young neighbours on the new housing estate in York. Michael and I could sometimes enjoy a coffee break together, and if I walked out with him in the afternoon, pushing the pram, I discovered that people really liked to meet the new curate's wife and that the old, housebound parishioners we visited were thrilled to have a peep at the curate's new baby. (Odd, isn't it, how it is always a *new* baby? I've never met an old one.)

As soon as Christopher was weaned at nine months, I decided to return to work. Every Monday afternoon I cycled two miles into the country to a chest hospital where, for three hours, I was no longer the curate's wife, but the medical social worker, sorting out the social problems of long stay TB patients and those with emphysema and lung cancer. The memory of a cross section of a lung blackened by cigarette smoking, displayed in the consultant's room, ensured that I was never tempted to smoke the weed. The other six hours, for which I was paid, were flexitime, and I used half to liaise with relatives, and half to do secretarial work.

I had spent two weeks in the August of 1960 blindfolded in Bournemouth. My sister Beryl, a trained secretary, had insisted that I should learn to touch-type and thus be able to produce my own dissertation for my degree and not have to pay a typist. Such a skill proved most valuable to me, as I progressed to type sermons, reports, essays, service sheets and inevitably the parish magazine.

In our earlier days, all I had to do was type the copy, which was collected by a dour, but obliging church member who ran a printing press. He returned it, expertly laid out and with a glossy cover, on a Friday. When he died, the church council made an unfortunate purchase - a second-hand ink duplicator with no instruction book. With this apparatus I had a hate/hate relationship, which threatened the stability of our family life.

I hated it because it was housed in one of our five icy attics and reduced me not only to tears but also to near-hypothermia.

I hated it because it was archaic, and represented the meanness of the church officials who guarded their considerable financial assets with zealous Yorkshire hard-business tenacity.

I hated it most of all because it was inefficient. It spewed out three of every five pages with bands of wet ink obliterating the words. Then, with venom, it spurted the remaining ink onto my clothes and hands and dyed them tar-black. The frustration at a locked up screen on my computer today is as a catapult compared with the cannon of fury unleashed at that duplicator. When I went from the parish I left it in splendid isolation in its attic, with a note that it was never to duplicate again.

There were other initiation rites through which I had to pass in an endeavour to become "a good vicar's wife". Not so much the wife of a good vicar, you understand, but a good "vicar's wife". Yes, this was to be my name for the next forty years.

I had started life as Margaret, been nicknamed Jaffa at school, and was called Miss Jefferson at University. For a while I was 'The Lady Almoner', or as one patient insisted – 'The Old Moaner'. I had so looked forward to being Mrs Walker, but rarely did this name feature; it was pushed out in favour of "the curate's wife", or "the vicar's wife". For a brief time I was "the rector's wife", but Joanna Trollope's novel had just been published, and I had to explain that, unlike her rector's wife, I was not likely to romp in fields with the archdeacon's brother. When Michael became Rural Dean, the assistant at the local tip was greatly impressed. As we approached with an estate car full of unsold jumble he would open the gates with a flourish, doff his hat, bow and say 'Good morning Mr Dean. Are you well Mrs Dean?' This I liked, and it made a change from my usual epithet. But apart from the odd reference to Christopher's mum, Pauline's mum or Rosie's mum, I had to sublimate my name in the interests of the Church.

As a curate's wife, I was fortunate in having a good vicar's wife to emulate. Pauline was a lovely, kind lady who found time between looking after a large vicarage, a conscientious husband, three very young children, and several parish organisations, to encourage me to join the Mothers' Union, to give votes of thanks, to form a special choir, and to launder the confirmation veils. This last task proved to be the most troublesome.

I knew she had high expectations. These veils were required to turn out as white as a seagull's undercarriage, starch-stiff, and crease-less. I lined up my attack : one bag of Reckitt's blue, a packet of Robin starch and my new Morphy Richards steam iron. Our single-tub washing-machine, which had cost £15 was very efficient, and as the black paddle started its monotonous half turn I confidently put in the fifteen squares of white cotton lawn, and left them to swirl in the near-boiling suds for twenty minutes while I went outside to sponge down the washing line.

Christopher, aged eleven months, was horizontally mobile. Born under the sign of Cancer, he was adept at a fast sideways crawl using his bottom and one hand. He had also mastered the skill of pulling himself up on the furniture, and had discarded the L-plates on his Baby-walker.

When I heard the ping of the washing machine timer I rushed into the kitchen and set the dial to stop. Off came the lid and 'voila'! There swam fifteen confirmation veils as green as, as green as...

... as green as Christopher's dungarees which rose to the surface like a dead Loch Ness monster. As I stood in paralytic panic I was jolted into action by a fully laden Baby-walker ramming into my heels. At the helm was my dungaree-less Baby Walker. He had come to see how his laundry was doing.

One hour, several rinses and a bottle of Domestos later I had almost restored the veils and my street-cred as an incipient five-star vicar's wife. I never confessed this incident to anyone, so had to feign surprise on hearing that when my successor laundered the veils the following year, they had started to disintegrate. Since then I have not doubted the claims of Domestos strength, but I have always delegated the task of veil-washing and concentrated on those things less fraught with peril.

Chapter 3

So, if laundering was not to be my gift to the Church, what was?

My mother was a piano teacher. I loved music and did not have to be coerced into playing the piano and violin. I had also had rudimentary instruction on the organ, so when there was an emergency at our first church, and the organist phoned to say he had the flu and didn't feel up to playing for the funeral which Michael was to take, I was happy to fill in.

At least, I was happy until the middle of the 23rd Psalm. Michael started in his usual strong, comforting voice, but then the green pastures started waving, and the still waters became choppy, as he plunged inexorably into the valley of the shadow of death in a loud fit of giggles. Appalled, I had no option but to lean out of the cocoon of the organ loft to see what had triggered this inappropriate behaviour. Then I saw **him** – our 18-month-old son crouching underneath the coffin in the chancel, popping out from behind the wreaths to shout, 'Boo – Daddy!'

I slid off the organ seat with a bass rumble, having forgotten I had the pedal stops on, and retrieved a terrified Christopher from the pin-striped arms of the chief undertaker who was holding the offending child with distaste, and hissing, 'nothing like this has ever happened to me before.' I whisked Christopher to the nearby vicarage, put him in the playroom and shot an arrow prayer to God to keep him safe while I rushed back to play the second hymn.

God obliged.

The cortège left for the crematorium. I was left to apologise to the remaining congregation and to explain why our young son had been brought to a funeral at all. We had, in fact, organised a baby-sitter, but on our way to deposit Christopher we had become stuck in a traffic jam. Realising we didn't have enough time to risk getting to the other side of York, we had reversed and gone straight to the church.

We had put him in the vestry, which had plenty of crèche toys, and asked the verger to nip round to keep an eye on him, once the cortège had arrived. We should have realised that Mr Trimble was incapable of 'nipping' round. He was in his eighties and was a plodder rather than a nipper.

Meanwhile, on hearing his daddy's voice, our little son had dragged a box to the vestry door, stood on it and pushed up the latch on the heavy door and, hey presto, let's play hide-and-seek under that big box with flowers on, and jump out to frighten daddy!

I played for no more funerals. Maybe weddings were more my scene.

It wasn't long before I had the chance to find out. The organist was going on holiday, so could I possibly play for a wedding in May? I could and I would. I made early arrangements for a baby-sitter to come to our house, and spent several happy hours on the organ stool, ensuring that sheep would safely graze, and that cool gales would fan the glade, where'er you walked. I experimented with trumpet and tuba stops for the *Wedding March*, and fairly blasted out the woodlice from their home beneath the foot pedals. All I had to do now was to meet the couple and hope that they would plump for Mendelssohn. If they insisted on Widor's *Toccata* I would have to resign. All was well. 'We'll have the usual,' they said, 'and just two hymns – *Guide Me O Thou Great Redeemer*, and *Love Divine*.' I wrote these down in my little book and looked forward to the tenth of May.

The wedding day dawned with rosy skies; the baby-sitter arrived early, and I walked excitedly to church. I wore a pink mini-skirt, which I thought suitable for a Spring wedding. The colour was certainly suitable, but the design was most certainly not. I had no wish to shock the elderly verger into an early grave, so I waited until he was well clear before I swung my legs onto the organ stool, revealing more flesh than befitted the curate's wife. Determined to provide good value for my two-guinea fee, I started to play at 11.20am in anticipation of the wedding at 12 noon. I was rather alarmed, therefore, to find that I had romped right through my repertoire in twenty minutes. Only the ushers had heard my first renditions, so after playing a few hymn tunes I launched into repertoire mark two. The congregation was so busy checking camera batteries and confetti supplies that I thought if I were to play *Three Blind Mice* or *The Happy Wanderer* nobody would notice, and I made a mental note to try this sometime and test my theory.

Right now, I had other things on which to concentrate. Michael had told me to keep an eye on the little light on the right of the organ which would flash green when the bride had arrived, signalling me to stop and await his announcement of the first hymn. The green light did not flash at 12 o'clock. I played some more hymn tunes. Ten minutes later and the groom and best man were straining their necks anxiously to the back of the church. I embarked on repertoire mark three.

At twenty past twelve, when I had just clocked up an hour's worth of playing, the green light flashed. I learned afterwards that the reason for the delay was that the wedding ring had somehow been put into a pocket of the groom's going-away suit, which was now in a case in a locker on York railway station. Saturday morning traffic was not conducive to rapid ring retrieval! In a relieved voice, Michael welcomed everyone to the church on this happy occasion and encouraged them to join in the first hymn. Heartily tired of sheep safely grazing, I attacked the hymn with gusto. The wedding guests started to sing, but with a distinct lack of enthusiasm, and by the time I had come to the end of the first verse I couldn't hear them singing at all, which was not surprising, as you will know if you have ever tried singing *Love divine, All Loves Excelling* to the tune of *Guide Me, O Thou Great Redeemer*. By the time I was onto *Bread of Heaven*, they had conceded defeat. Before I ventured onto verse two, Michael intervened and shouted to me, 'You're playing the wrong tune!' to which I retorted, 'I'm sorry, but you've announced the wrong hymn.'

The wedding couple, it appeared, had given me the hymns in one order, and then had them printed in the reverse order on the service sheet. The ushers had been so busy on ring retrieval duties that they had failed to provide me with the sheet, which Michael was now waving under my nose to prove his point. '*Love Divine*, here we come!'

The vows were made, the itinerant ring was produced, and I hoped that everyone would now have forgotten the hymn debacle.

While the registers were being signed I played soft music and prepared again for the green light's flash. It came. I triumphantly pulled out the trumpet stop and crashed into the *Wedding March*. Everyone stood up and peered expectantly to the arch leading from the vestry to the chancel. No one emerged. I knew the registers had been signed because I'd seen the photographer gather his tripod and leap down the side aisle to be ready at the west door, so I kept on playing. As it became obvious that there was no action imminent I reluctantly pushed in the trumpet stop and transferred to a funereal rendering of Handel's *Largo*, which had the capability of being dragged out indefinitely, and the congregation slid back onto their pews, in bewilderment.

The green light flashed again. Or was I now in such a highly wrought state that I was imagining it? Michael confirmed that all was now ready, and as my second attempt at the *Wedding March* blasted out, the guests arose, and the bridal procession moved down the aisle and into the sunshine.

'What on earth were you doing in the vestry all that time?' I demanded, when I had played my last note, and switched off the blower.

'You might well ask', replied my strained looking husband.

Apparently there was a wrought iron grid over the heating pipes in the vestry, and as the procession had lined up for their grand exit, the bride's stiletto heel had gone through the grating. She had fallen over, the bridesmaid had fallen on top of her, thus wrenching the tiara off the bride's head, and ripping the veil. Michael had had to cope with hysterics from them both, pull the heel from the grate, and then do running repairs to the tiara and veil, using hairgrips!

'And what were you doing, messing up that first hymn?' he threw out at me, in an attempt to pass the buck.

Hopefully all the guests were posing for photos by this time, and only the verger was witness to our combined wrath.

'You're not playing for any more of my weddings!'

'Don't worry', I shouted, 'I wouldn't even play for your funeral!'

By the time I ventured onto an organ seat again, the days of the mini-skirt had long since passed.

Chapter 4

If you have a good recipe for brains, do let me know.

Yes, I know fish is good for the brain. This was just as well, as our second curacy was to be in dockland Hull. Fish was our staple diet, as we tried to live on a salary of £500 a year, with a two-year-old son and another baby on the way. What I needed was a way of producing brains on toast – that creamy white delicacy which my mother had served up to me as a child in the Second World War. Knowing of our need to economise, our butcher in Hull sold me a sheep's head for a shilling, but I had not succeeded in convincing the family that the resultant grey sludge sitting on the perfect toast was edible, let alone nutritious. Reluctantly I turned my attention to my projected book, *Margaret's Million Meals with Mince.*

Mince and money had to be stretched a great deal in the mid-1960s. There were four churches in the large parish. Three were 'daughter churches' built in the midst of vast housing estates which had mushroomed in post-war years. The fourth was the small parish church, once a village church, but now surrounded by industry, wasteland, a Jewish cemetery and the docks. Next door was an imposing brick Edwardian vicarage, and it was here that we lived for three years, while the vicar, a bachelor, chose to live in one of the curates' houses. We had to furnish and try to heat it, so some of our wedding presents had to be sold to keep us solvent. As Christmas approached, we parted company with an antique Victorian fire screen, with its adjustable shield shape designed to protect delicate skin from the fire. Pregnant, and battling with a push-chair on the road by the docks in a force seven Easterly wind blowing from the Urals, I never felt the need to protect my face from the warmth of the welcome vicarage fire. As we tucked into a large capon on Christmas Day, and joint of pork on Boxing Day, we added to our Grace 'Thank you God for the donor of the departed fire screen!'

In York, I had enjoyed the companionship of other young families on the new housing estate where we had lived in a normal semi-detached house. In Hull, I was much more isolated, and found life more difficult. Michael's work seemed to consist of baptisms, weddings and funerals, which came in staggering numbers. The baby bulge of 1947 was doing its own baby-bulging twenty years later. In York, Michael had occasionally had as many as four baptisms at any one service. In Hull there were often 15 or 16, and they were noisy affairs. That is, until Michael took charge.

Babies about to be baptised know there is something afoot. They are taken out of their normal routine, hurriedly fed while mother fills the vol-au-vents, dressed in stiff white gowns and bonnets, then handed around the motley relatives, and finally taken into a cold church with a loud organ. The final ignominy is to be handed over to a strange man, dressed like a woman, who proceeds to pour cold water over their heads. No wonder they scream. Early in our Hull days, Michael held the first squawking baby over his shoulder and felt the bubble of air, which was giving rise to windy pains. Being an experienced father by now, he sent a choirboy over to the vicarage for some gripe water, and proceeded to spoon it into the open-mouthed child. Like all babies, it had a taste for the alcoholic content, and glugged it down with obvious satisfaction and soon produced both the desired belch, and the undesired contents of its lunch down Michael's newly-ironed surplice. All the other mothers wanted gripe water for their crying infants. The result was a quiet service, and an empty bottle of Nurse Harvey's when

I wanted it for our baby later that evening. At the next parish office session, mothers were asking 'Can we have our Charlie done next month, and can we have the fellow who gives the gripe water?' Not wanting the expense of a monthly bottle of gripe water, or of encouraging addiction in ones so young, Michael developed a new technique of calming at the font.

If you ever see him baptise today you will note that this still works. Firstly, he wraps the baby tightly round with the shawl which great-aunt Nellie has knitted in laborious two-ply. Then, he hoists it over his left shoulder, leaving his right hand free to turn over pages, light candles, and pour water into the font. He then applies light pressure on the baby's back with his large left hand, while doing a sudden knees-bend motion. This catches the baby on the hop. It immediately stops crying and opens its beautiful blue eyes wide in wonderment and gazes adoringly into his face. After a few baby-cooing words he proceeds to baptise the baby, who by now seems impervious to the trickling water, and remains mute until handed back into the less secure arms of the young godmother.

The parents are full of gratitude to the calming curate, and invite us to the baptism tea, where Michael often ends up standing in a corner performing his knees-bend routine, with the baby over his shoulder (his cassock now in the firing line), while I ply him with salmon sandwiches and the hastily filled vol-au-vents which had caused the trouble in the first place!

Churching, or the thanksgiving for a safe delivery in childbirth, was already on the decline in England, but for many it was a superstitious affair, and seafarers are well known for erring on the side of caution in this respect. I suspect that parishes in ports saw the last vestiges of this service.

One bitterly cold Saturday night, when the East Coast November fog had penetrated up the Humber and muted the street lights, we had just gone up to bed when we heard a motorbike splutter to a halt and the sound of feet scrunching up our gravel drive. A young man in full leathers asked if his wife could be 'churched.' Michael said that was no problem – there would be a churching service before the baptisms the following afternoon. But this was not good enough – he wanted it done now – at five past eleven, and led Michael down the drive. 'He won't do it tonight, Doreen,' he mouthed through the flimsy Perspex windows of the sidecar where his wife and four-day-old son were huddled beneath a tartan rug.

Apparently Doreen was desperate to have a bath but her mother-in-law wouldn't let her across the threshold until she'd been churched, as this would have brought bad luck on the family. Sympathetic to their plight, but not willing to do the churching, if it was seen only as a superstitious ceremony, Michael offered the services of the vicarage bathroom. By the time I had dressed and found clean towels, the motor-bike was revving up and 'unclean Doreen' and her tiny bundle were receding into the mist. We should really have telephoned the neighbouring vicar to prepare him for a late night call.

For winter baptisms I used to boil a kettle of water to be taken over to church. Poured into the font before the service, it was just at a pleasant tepid temperature to land on the child's forehead. One Sunday I decanted the hot water into a plastic jug. As Michael ran over to church, a vicious East wind whipped the top off the jug and drenched his trousers with water. He decided, unwisely, that he had no time to come home to change. He continued his journey to church by which time the water had frozen and he felt very uncomfortable, but not half as uncomfortable as he did later in the service when the warmth of the radiator near the font worked its charms, and the icy patches began to melt with telltale drips. Maybe at the next baptism-booking session they would ask for a curate who wasn't incontinent!

Chapter 5

'Holy, Holy, Holy, The Lord God Almighty', painted in red and gold, looked down from the chancel arch onto all family rituals, onto the white-bonneted babies at the font and onto the flower-bedecked coffins laid on their black trestles.

The happiest occasions, though, peaked in spring. In this large parish with its vast housing estates there seemed to be a continuous procession of weddings, and in the 1960s many couples wanted to marry in March in a bid to beat the taxman. Consequently we had as many as eleven weddings a Saturday in the early spring – a challenge not only for the parson but also for the organist. The obvious solution was for the vicar to take two weddings, with me playing the organ, and for Michael to take the next two weddings accompanied by the 'proper' organist, and so on. This arrangement meant that one or other of us was always at home to look after our children as we did our continuous changeover throughout those happy March Saturdays, producing, hopefully, happy married couples every three-quarters of an hour.

Sometimes guests had to be asked to take their feet off the pews in front, or to stop smoking. One bride's father was obviously so nervous that he forgot to remove his cap before proudly taking his daughter up the aisle. My rendition of *Here Comes the Bride* (sorry Wagner, but Lohengrin doesn't have a look in), was abruptly halted as the bride's mother shouted down the aisle, "'enry, take your 'at off and start again!'

Outside the church there was a merry intermingling of wedding guests, as the couple who had just come out of church posed for photos at the right-hand side of the lychgate, and the bridegroom and best man of the next wedding were manoeuvred into place at the left hand side. This was a far cry from 21st century weddings when the filming lasts four times as long as the ceremony, and receptions start five hours after the service! Nowadays, there is great scope for an enterprising Mothers' Union to set up in the business of 'interim snacks' for tummy-rumbling guests who have probably set off before daybreak and not even had a proper breakfast.

In our dockland parish we had many seafarers, few of whom felt it worthwhile to own a car, so parking around the church wasn't the problem you might have supposed, as most guests opted to come in the free double-decker bus, laid on by the bride's family. Only when two of these coincided did the fun begin, as they waltzed around each other in 11-point turns in the narrow lane leading to the church. Inside the church we had our fair share of fun and games, too. There was the groom who couldn't write – not even his own name. In an effort to protect him from embarrassment in front of his new in-laws, Michael wrote the name on a piece of paper and guided his hand as he copied it. Then there was the bride whose engagement ring flew off in the vestry and dropped behind a large built-in cupboard. Michael coped with her hysterics and promised to have the ring ready for her on her return from honeymoon. The following Monday he devoted most of his day off to unscrewing and lifting the cupboard to retrieve the sapphire-and-diamond ring, giving it to me to wear on my wedding finger for safe keeping. Six weeks later, the bride had not collected it; she was waiting for us to return it! I was cross at the time, and even now I blame Michael's subsequent hernia onto that thankless ring retrieval.

However, there was one positive outcome. I had become so used to wearing a third ring, that, when I had to hand it over, my finger felt quite naked. The following Christmas Michael bought me a sapphire-and-diamond ring. 'Is this a replacement?' I asked. 'No, it's a maternity ring!' he said in all innocence. As I endured the long wait for our second child I realised he was right. Maternity does seem like Eternity!

Pauline was born at home on a March Saturday. No, I wasn't on organ-playing duty that day, and did manage to produce her in between two of the weddings allotted to Michael. He strode in to the next wedding on a high and proudly announced to the guests that he now had a daughter, weighing ten-and-a-half pounds. As I am only just over five feet tall, it was no wonder I had looked like the sides of the wedding buses which were even now revving up outside the vicarage.

Rest, after my exertions, was short-lived, as the following Sunday was Palm Sunday and the four churches needed five hundred palm crosses making up from palm leaves. Guess who was deemed to have nothing better to do? Don't ever be tempted to take your carefully folded palm cross to bits to see if you can put it together again. You can't! It is a skill which you acquire only when you have wasted the first ten which have been folded in the wrong place, or which have split as you poke the last bit through the crux. Each Palm Sunday I stand for the blessing of the palms and recall how many times I had blessed them in a rather different way in those wrongly named 'lying-in' days, when I should have been reclining on a frilly pillow gazing adoringly at my daughter and receiving grapes and flowers.

Grapes and flowers are, in most churches, the mainstay of harvest decorations. Not so in this parish, dominated by the sea and ancillary industries. Fishing nets were draped between pillars, and neat bottles of cod liver oil graced one window ledge. In the next were tiny tins of paint – the envy of all model makers, including Michael who had a model railway in the vicarage attics. Christopher, meanwhile, insisted on sitting by the front window where, standing majestically, was a large model crane which actually worked and kept him occupied in post-harvest days until the man from the crane factory came to take it away until the following year.

The church was small, having been built originally to serve a village, rather than the sprawling network of housing estates which now spread out their tentacles ever eastwards. It had no particular architectural merit, and was urgently in need of a thorough spring-clean – the last major one having been in 1943 – presumably done by the ladies while their men were engaged in the war. Now, in 1968, Brownies, Mothers' Union, Ladies' Fellowship and the Sunday school all turned out to do their bit, and the walls began to reveal an unexpected cream-colour beneath the grey grime. At the end of the day, we realised that it might have been better to have started at the top and worked down. The next day the men brought ladders and worked hard, but their rivulets of grime snaked down onto the ladies' pristine lower walls. Yes, we should have started at the top.

Some stains were so stubborn that a local publican offered us the use of a strong spray, which he used to deal with nicotine stains. This was powerful stuff and made light work of the chancel arch top. I left Michael and helpers to it, and went back to the vicarage to make coffee. Before the kettles had boiled I was despatched post-haste on my bike to deliver an urgent message. 'Tell the vicar that the Lord God Almighty is running!' The powerful chemicals had run down into the red and gold lettering of 'Holy, Holy, Holy, Lord God Almighty' and were rapidly putting my husband's chances of promotion down to an all-time low. Having delivered the message to an ashen-faced vicar, I returned to find that Christopher had occupied himself, oh so quietly, by prising out pieces of mosaic in the sanctuary. It was at this point that we heard of the death of a former churchwarden. His funeral was to be on Good Friday morning – just three days hence. While Michael and his men mopped up the Lord God, I devoted my energies to restoring the mosaic floor – the equivalent of doing a five hundred piece jigsaw most of which is sky. The vicar looked on with a grim expression, and I knew our time in this parish was coming to an end.

Perhaps my saving grace was that, in the absence of a vicar's wife, I had agreed to lead the Mothers' Union meetings. Unlike the Ladies' Fellowship who were liberal with swear words and boasted of their husband's prowess in stealing items from the docks, the Mothers' Union was an older brigade, who sported magnificent hats on festival occasions. I was 40 years younger than their average age, so was understandably nervous when asked to take the chair at a large Deanery meeting, with over a hundred ladies present. The vicar, suitably relieved that I was to lead the meeting, volunteered to take charge of the tea arrangements, and busied himself behind the hatch setting out cups and saucers and watching the urn. Just before I announced the visiting speaker, the bachelor vicar poked his head from the hatch doors and asked if he could interrupt for just one minute. 'Ladies', he asked, 'how many of you are sterilised?' My bright red suit was no match for my cheeks, as I shared his embarrassment. He was, in fact, referring to the kind of milk to be poured into the teacups. For many ladies it was not a proper cup unless its milk came from one of those tall bottles with a metal cap.

We had gone to this parish to get experience. It had served us well. With the benefit of hindsight I know I could have done better. However, some 35 years after leaving, we returned for the Silver wedding of Catherine, one of the young Sunday school teachers from our days there, and were heartened to see a thriving church, led by some who had been in the Youth Club in our time there in the late 1960s. We sat in the congregation with them. The Lord God Almighty, who had long since stopped running, looked down on us, and, knowing all things, blessed us.

Chapter 6

Praise to the Lord, the Almighty, the King of Creation is still my favourite hymn. We had sung it at our wedding, at the baptisms of our two babies, and were now about to sing it at Michael's induction as a vicar in Halifax. We believed that our hearts' wishes had so far been granted in what he ordaineth, but I was not sure about this move to Halifax. After all, the beggar's litany reads 'From Hull, Hell and Halifax, Good Lord deliver us.' We'd been to Hull, hoped to escape Hell, but were now being called to serve in Halifax.

I didn't want to go to the West Riding. I was a native of Beverley, the capital of the East Riding. I viewed anything that came from the West Riding with suspicion. As a child I used to go on summer Sunday train excursions to Bridlington with my mum and dad. As soon as we had spread out our tartan rug on the sand, we would be invaded on the beach by hordes of West Riding families, as they set up their encampments with near-military zeal. The ladies, seated in hilariously erected deckchairs, watched as the men battled with green canvas bathing tents, and the children scoured the beach for large stones to weigh down the tents' inside pockets. The barricade of windscreens completed the corral, inside which grandmas knitted, grandpas had their feet buried in sand and pushchairs were rocked by crooning mothers. Meanwhile, fathers were marking out the pitch for the morning cricket match, which went on until the lure of egg sandwiches, crisps in greaseproof bags with blue twists of salt, and lemonade called them in.

As a child I felt intimidated by these alien Yorkshiremen and boys with different accents, although I did envy their camaraderie, and felt a momentary touch of warmth towards them if I was invited to field on the long-on boundary to save the fours. At half past five, the long trek started back to the railway station, where rows of West-Riding-ites tentacled round the outside of the station. Inside I would wait my turn behind queues of boys, clutching my two pennies to put in a machine which had a big dial and one arrow hand. Twenty-two twists and thumps later and out would come a metal strip with the letters of my name embossed. It read either Dorothy Margaret Jeffe, or DorothyMargaretJeffers if I omitted the spaces. The next time I came to Bridlington I would remember to leave out the Dorothy, and then I could have Margaret Jefferson in her entirety. Meanwhile I trudged to the excursion platform bearing my sharp metal strip, trying to think what on earth I could use it for, while the station announcer directed trainloads of sandy children and their families to Bradford, Leeds, Huddersfield, Batley and Halifax. They were returning to dark millstone grit, to breathe in smoke from belching mill chimneys while I was free to soak in the fresh East Coast breezes wafting over golden cornfields.

So that was why I didn't want to go to Halifax.

I imagined the church and vicarage would be soot-grimed from the Victorian industrial revolution.

I was right. They were.

I had realised when I married Michael that I might have to go to places which I didn't relish. You can argue with your husband, but it is more difficult to argue with God. As if to sweeten the pill, the sun shone from a clear blue sky on the day I first saw the parish. The church and vicarage stood majestically at the corner of a wonderful expanse of grassland, known as 'The Moor', which rolled down to a promenade, above attractive rocky woodland facing the invigorating Pennines. The air was fresh and bracing. Halifax was a smokeless zone now. My nappies would stay white and smut free. It would be exciting to live in such a big house. Which of the two huge front rooms would I have as the lounge? My imagination was ahead of its time. There were other applicants for the job.

The only question Michael remembers from his interview with the trustees of the living is 'Can you sing?' Fortunately he was truthful and confessed that after several years of tuition from me he could usually get the Lord to open his lips on an approximate 'G'. This answer obviously impressed them, as they realised that in this parish, which had a very high profile musical tradition, it might not be a good idea to have a very musical vicar who would run the risk of major conflict with organists and choirmasters.

He got the job.

The day of the induction was wild and wet. Hailstones battered at the church clock-face and stopped the clock. I was busy doing last-minute things in the vicarage before the service started, so my sister preceded me to church. The verger thought she was the new vicar's wife so she was ushered to an exalted seat. When I made my grand entrance with three minutes to go, I was slotted in half-way down the aisle, and as I was comforting myself with the biblical precedent of taking the lower seat, sure enough I was called up higher!

Previous incumbents' wives had been older and more sophisticated than me. Some had even had private means and been able to afford live-in maids. It must have been a shock for the congregation, therefore, to find that the latest one was only 29, had children of four and two, and wore, for the induction, a mini-length turquoise coat revealing quite a bit of leg. I loved this coat – bought from Thornton-Varley's in Hull at a cost of £27/6d. Did I imagine the internal tut-tuttings of the older ladies as they observed my hem-line? Did I discern an unexpected interest from the men-folk? Certainly one rather unkempt man made a point of introducing himself to me four times during the course of the bun-fight after the service. He was very anxious that I should remember who he was, and assured me he would be a frequent caller at the vicarage. I thought he must be an eminent member of the Church Council – probably an eccentric retired professor - though I did wonder why, on the fourth encounter, he gave me his inside-leg measurements. After the usual welcome speeches I found myself assuring various people that I was a Mothers' Union member, and yes, of course I would come to the magazine distributors' meeting, and that I would try to set up a Sunday morning crèche as top priority. Eventually I had the opportunity to ask the churchwarden about my strange man. No, he wasn't a mad professor. He was a gentleman of the road who called at the vicarage for sandwiches, and frequented the parish jumble sales when he needed new clothes. Hence the importance of my knowing he needed 32-inch inside-leg trousers!

I was soon to realise that the social work training I had had could be put to good use at the vicarage door. It wasn't only tramps that came, but anxious mothers to book baptisms, nervous couples wanting to plan their weddings, the bereaved, the disturbed, and the lonely, who wanted someone to listen. If Michael wasn't in, or was busy dealing with someone else, I had the task of inviting them in, making them a drink, and listening to their stories. For some I was doing 'a holding operation' until they could see the vicar. Others, I think, may have appreciated the chance to talk to a woman, albeit one who wore mini-skirts!

Sometimes, when the phone went or the doorbell rang, just as I was putting the children to bed, I cursed under my breath. When I confessed this to an older and wiser vicar's wife she gave me a valuable piece of advice. 'Your ministry' she said, 'may be that of a ministry of interruptions.' Over the years I came to appreciate this. In my youth I thought I knew what God wanted me to do each day, and resented interruptions to the tasks in hand. In hindsight I realise that it was in dealing with the situations that I deemed 'interruptions' that I was more likely to be doing what God really wanted.

One job I relished was helping Michael on a Sunday afternoon. As well as being a parish priest, Michael was also part-time chaplain to the local hospital. He really enjoyed his ward visits as well as taking Communion to the patients each Sunday morning, and leading services on different wards in the afternoon. Having worked in hospitals myself I quite envied his right of entry, and was therefore very glad when a parishioner volunteered to have the children to tea on a Sunday so that I could go with Michael to play the organ for the ward service.

To begin with, this involved playing a decrepit piano, most of whose keys were stiff or unplayable, largely due to the fact that the piano top was seen as a depository for at least eight flower vases. Flower water and musical instruments do not mix! The League of Friends then bought an electronic organ with a heavy wooden case on castors which could be trundled up and down the corridor to the wards. I remember Michael coming home after giving a lecture on the role of the hospital chaplain to the new intake of nursing students. When instructing them on their involvement in the ward services he was somewhat surprised to find them rolling around with laughter. It was only on reflection that he realised that he had said, 'You'll know when I'm coming to your ward for a service when you see me coming down the corridor pushing my organ in front of me.'

My first venture as ward organist didn't fare much better. I had a pretty good idea of what hymns the ladies would like. They usually chose school favourites, or wedding hymns. Top of the pops was *The Lord's my Shepherd*, sung to *Crimond*, followed closely by *Praise my soul* and *Lead us Heavenly Father, Lead Us*. However, my first service was on a men's ward.

'Choose something strong and virile', said Michael. I did just that. Around me on Male Orthopaedic, were men on crutches, men with knees padded after cartilage operations, men with legs in plaster, limbs held up high on traction. The hymn I chose? *Stand up, stand up for Jesus*.

Chapter 7

I like hymns. They were the first things I learned to play on the piano. I grew up on a regular diet of church-going and hymn-singing as my dad was churchwarden and treasurer, and my mum was superintendent of the Infants' Sunday school at our East Riding church. She also played the organ for funerals. Every Sunday after evensong, the tall, young priest-in-charge would come round to our house. He liked to play duets on the piano with my mum, and he liked to play hymns. He was a bachelor, and I think he also liked my mum's cheese-straws and egg custards.

In those days most churches had 'Ancient and Modern' – the original fat, black edition, long before the maroon 'Ancient and Modern Revised' or bright red 'New Standard' reared their cheery faces. It was a pity my mum and the curate were not sponsored, for I think they played every hymn in the book over the course of those winter Sunday evenings in the 1950s. Many of them I knew from Sunday services, but there were lesser-known ones with memorable opening lines such as 'Within the churchyard side by side lay many long low graves'. But among some of the dross were hidden gems. When we reached number 500, there we found a lovely tune, with words that purported to be about the Springtime, but, as I learned later, were based on the erotic Song of Solomon – 'Rise up my love my fair one, arise and come away.' My dad sang it with enthusiasm. He sang most things with enthusiasm – including naughty words to the tune of *The Church's one Foundation*. I think he'd learned them in the First World War. My mum was embarrassed when he mouthed them to me at evensong, and when he spat out his 't's in *Light at Evening Time*. The spindrift of his saliva landed neatly on the fox-head fur of Mrs MacManus whose solid frame occupied the end place in the pew in front. I hated that fox-head whose beady eyes stared at me through the sermon. They deserved my father's spit on them.

My hymn knowledge was extended firstly by our school hymnbook, *Songs of Praise*, which added *Daisies are our Silver, Buttercups our Gold* and *Glad that I live Am I* to my repertoire. At university, the Anglican Society went to different churches in Nottingham each Sunday, and the Christian Association worshipped with different denominations, so, apart from our visits to the Quakers, when all I could hear was the rumbling of my friend's stomach, I learned many new hymns from the Wesley, Sankey and Moody stables. My growing knowledge of hymnody was to stand me in good stead as a vicar's wife.

Some organists and choirmasters like to choose the hymns themselves; others feel it is the vicar's job. Although it is easier to go along with whatever the organist chooses, it does make sense for the vicar to draw up the service outline and suggest hymns based on that Sunday's theme. This job was soon delegated to me, and to begin with I revelled at the challenge of finding hymns to link with the Church's season, the collect, epistle or gospel, the tenor of the sermon, and any current world events. This proved much more difficult than I had ever imagined. Very soon I realised that hymns are highly emotive. I also realised that most people in the congregation had a very limited hymn repertoire, and were not overly keen on extending it. They were also apt to go into decline if *O Jesus, I Have Promised* was played to the tune *Wolvercote* when they had always sung it to *Thornbury*, and were liable to massacre the hymn-chooser, if (God forbid) she had set it to *Day of Rest* or even more radically, to *Hatherop Castle* from *20ᵗʰ Century Hymns*.

On the more positive side it was rewarding to introduce new hymns to a parish and to see them become established favourites. I soon learned that it was a case of *'festina lente'*; not more than one new one a month, and never choose it as the first or last hymn. Better to sandwich it somewhere in the middle, and send them the congregation out on *Cwm Rhondda* rather than risk a riot.

Helping couples choose their wedding hymns was usually an occasion to be savoured. Very few came to the vicarage for their pre-wedding interview with a clear-cut list of the music they wanted. Some were clearly under their parents' thumbs and appeared to have no say in the matter themselves. Others knew only the hymns they could remember from school, not all of which were appropriate. I apologise if you had *Morning has Broken*, or *Lord of the Dance* at your wedding, but I really can't see that they have any connection with marriage. William Blake would, I think, have been very surprised to know that *Jerusalem* was in the Top Ten list for weddings, not only in England's green and pleasant land, but also in our subsequent parishes in Wales. Apart from its request for arrows of desire, I could see no other possible wedding links. While appreciating that it was 'their wedding' and they could choose what they liked, within reason, I did try veering couples off *Fight the Good Fight* – suggesting it was not an appropriate start to their married life. Neither did I encourage as the hymn following the vows, *Dear Lord and Father of mankind, forgive our foolish ways*. Were they regretting already the step they had just taken?

One couple in Hull presented me with a crumpled pencil-written list, entitled "Hims wat we want". Their first request was *Immoral, Invisible*. I am sure "God only wise" would understand! They then proceeded to tell me what they wanted playing during the signing of the register. They spoke in unison and they spoke very quickly. I shall never forget their swift joined-up outpouring of 'awitershaydoperl'. I looked perplexed and they repeated it at an even faster tempo. 'You know – everyone has it nowadays.' I was in my late twenties and had two small children and I realised I was now obviously out-of-touch with the current musical scene. Too embarrassed to say I had never heard of a piece with this strange title, I took the coward's way out and said I would see what I could do. The church Youth Club members took one look at my phonetically-spelt title and shrieked, 'A Whiter Shade of Pale'. I nodded sagely, and said, 'of course!' I had never heard of it, but managed to procure a copy, and now I will never forget it. It is filed away along with other once-off requests to be played at weddings and funerals – *One step at a time*, *Candle in the Wind*, and *I'll do it My Way*. The only request Michael turned down was for *Smoke Gets in your Eyes*. Not to be outdone, the deceased's son played it - at the crematorium!

Our children grew up with a wide knowledge of the world and the diversity of its inhabitants, and they were quite au fait with the vocabulary of death. 'It's the undertaker on the phone, dad – can you do a burial on Tuesday?' Once, in the middle of Pauline's seventh birthday party, Michael took a phone call while at the tea table. Only Pauline kept on munching her sandwiches, while Michael muttered 'When did she die?' and 'Is it to be burial or crem?' The other eight little girls sat silent and wide-eyed. When Michael left to go to the study to check his diary, Pauline immediately satisfied their curiosity by giving them a burner-by-burner account of the workings of the crematorium right down to the final ash in the casket. I don't think anyone wanted jelly and blancmange after that. Except Pauline!

Undertakers of our acquaintance were unfailingly polite and friendly. The one I remember best rejoiced in the splendid name of 'Mr Boddy'. His usual greeting was 'Good afternoon. Boddy here. I've got another one for you.' The children and I became funeral-competent, quickly asking salient questions as to the deceased's name, address, age, next of kin, date and time of burial/crem, charities to which donations would be given, and venue of the funeral nosh. In Yorkshire they were traditionally buried with ham. I had to remember to cut down on husband's lunch or tea provisions if he had been to a funeral tea. Maybe he kept a little notebook of funeral caterers; he certainly knew who made the best mushroom vol-au-vents and chocolate éclairs. Anyone browsing his diary would have thought that his life was one long stream of merrymaking: Fun at 11am on Monday, Fun 2pm Tuesday and Fun 12 noon Thursday. Or maybe he was into bread, for on Sundays he had Baps at 2pm and did his Bap preparation on Friday at 6pm. Maybe I should arm future writers of his biography with a book of most commonly used abbreviations.

Even computer spell-checkers wouldn't have quibbled with his abbreviations. Neither would they have picked up my typing errors. Getting the parish magazine out in time meant that I was usually under pressure, and my mind flew ahead of my fingers. Or was it a Freudian slip, some might wonder, when the vicar's letter was addressed to 'My dear fiends.'

'There was a pretty good turn out for a wet February Sunday evening,' commented Michael. Maybe it was because I had whetted their appetites with the prospect of evensnog at 6.30pm! Maybe this inspired another parish to advertise 'Matings at 10.30am.' I was not alone in parish magazine misprints. One afternoon, after speaking at a meeting in our neighbouring parish, I was drinking my tea, when I was aware of hilarity in the kitchen, where the tea ladies had just received their bundles of newsletters to deliver. One lady was having a quick read-through when she collapsed with mirth at what the young vicar had written: 'Would all mothers wanting babies please come to the parish office at 7pm and not to the vicarage.' The Mothers' Union were soon armed with pens to insert the word 'baptised' between the words 'babies' and 'please' in 500 newsletters before the parish office was besieged or the vicar defrocked!

Early on I learned that proofreading should be done by someone else. It is so easy to be blind to your own mistakes. Yet when asked to proofread someone else's copy I can nit-pick like a frantic monkey. I seem to remember Jesus having words to say about planks and specks of sawdust!

Chapter 8

'You've a big house to follow,' said the Halifax parishioners to me. 'You've a big job to follow,' they intoned in the same breath to Michael. We nodded in agreement, hoping this was the correct response. We had nightmares of chasing elusive vicarages and congregations, and never catching them up. Apparently the West Riding interpretation of 'to follow' can roughly be translated 'to look after'. As I followed the trail of books in the study, children's toys in the living room and dropped socks and pants in the bedrooms I could see that I had quite a family to follow.

The parish, although very modestly sized compared to our Hull one, nevertheless took a lot of following. The church and vicarage, solid in Victorian millstone grit, shared their campus with a modern church hall which was home to a pre-school playgroup, Brownies, Guides, Darby & Joan, Mothers' Union, and Men's Fellowship, as well as hosting Diocesan and Deanery meetings and many of the town's charity coffee mornings and children's parties. The congregation was young and enthusiastic and eager to move forward. It was immediately obvious to us that "to whom much is given, much is expected". It also became clear that being a vicar was quite different from being a curate. The buck stopped sooner.

Michael was soon engrossed in his joint role of vicar and hospital chaplain. Christopher had started school, and Pauline was enrolled into the playgroup for three mornings a week. I suspected that some people were wondering if I was now going to "get a job". Did they not reckon that following this lively parish, a 15-roomed vicarage, a busy husband and two small children constituted enough of a job for a young woman not yet 30? It wasn't the obvious duties that took the time – it was the unrelenting telephone with funeral details to be taken down, baptism visits to be arranged, and sometimes upset parishioners to be appeased. Then there were the NFAs. As a former hospital almoner I had studied a compendium of oft-used abbreviations before being allowed onto the wards on my first day. I remember my ghoulish delight in learning new acronyms. BID and DOT (brought in dead, and died on table). I also recall the tale of a patient expected to be next in the queue for orthopaedic outpatients. He had looked at his card on which was written POP off. So he did. How long he had the plaster of Paris on his leg before returning to the hospital I know not. I do know that as an almoner I often dealt with NFAs – gentleman (or ladies) of the road, and of No Fixed Abode.

Our vicarage, situated next to the church and not far from the hospital was on the Western approach to the town. This was an obvious attraction to the tramps who always seemed to be travelling West to East from Ireland or Liverpool or Manchester, and who, on reaching Yorkshire, always decided they wanted to have their return fare paid by a young and seemingly naïve young vicar's wife. I heard enough bad luck stories to make all my hankies sodden; I had also had 'tramp training' in my social work days. Even so it was not easy to square my refusal to give money with the Gospel teaching 'to lend, hoping for nothing again …' Only once in our ministry did we ever recoup money lent to those who came begging at the vicarage door. To get this back Michael visited a council house on a Hull estate every week for ten weeks, returning with two shillings each time. On his final visit the man's wife gave him tea and cakes and a profuse thank you for restoring her husband's resolve to "go straight" and stop lying.

Mindful of St. Matthew's words on seeing the hungry, the thirsty, the naked, the stranger and the prisoner, and not turning away, we always offered food and drink and, if necessary, clothes to those who turned up on the vicarage doorstep, and we stood for many minutes listening to their stories. Occasionally my giving went too far. Michael had received a letter summoning him to see the archbishop so decided he had better rake out his best suit and look smart. 'Where are my braces?' he shouted down. 'These trousers won't stay up without them.' I had to confess that I had given them to a tramp the day before, along with his gardening trousers. Michael visited Bishopthorpe with an unwieldy nappy pin holding him together. Somewhere a tramp was tramping westwards in newly-acquired trousers held up by new blue braces.

Life was full and never dull. I enjoyed the variety of each day and vainly hoped that people arriving on the vicarage doorstep were pleased to find a 'non-working vicar's wife' there rather than to have to keep on returning until the vicar was in. (By the way, if ever you want an example of an oxymoronic phrase, then look no further than "a non-working vicar's wife"). I was not tempted to seek paid employment, but if anyone asked, 'do you work?' I answered with an emphatic YES!

The vicarage had been built in 1895, five years after the church. In those days there may have been a coachman, and there most certainly were maids, whose quarters were in the icy attics, and who used the back stairs. A network of bells ran round all the rooms. Alas, by 1969 the system was not linked up. Alas, also, there was no resident maid. Until my predecessor's reign, there had been a live-in help. In my early days in Halifax, in the days when I tried to clean the huge outside windows myself, I was perched at the top of a rather precarious set of steps, wielding an aerosol spray, when the postman shouted, 'Will you take these in to your mistress?' Descending from my top step as modestly as I could in a mini-skirt, and with as much dignity as I could muster, I announced, 'I am the mistress!' With obvious disbelief he proceeded to the front door and dropped the post through the letterbox. I was not to be trusted.

I soon realised the folly of trying to wash the windows. Not being able to afford a window cleaner, I abandoned the outside glass to the force of the frequent Pennine rainstorms, and concentrated on the insides. Because the house stood on a prominent mound on a busy corner, we had to have net curtains to maintain some privacy. Thirty-six net curtains. Four times a year I would have a net-washing week, and take them down six at a time, fold them into small squares and dunk them in suds, then rinse, unfold and peg on the line. This way they needed no ironing. After six days I had completed the task, with no muddling up of which went where. Washing was one of my favourite household jobs, and I loved to see a full washing-line billowing in the reliable West Riding west wind.

Best of all was a line of nappies. Pauline had been out of nappies for nearly three years. We still had the pram, the cot, the residue of the 58 matinee coats and cardigans that the York parishioners had knitted for Christopher, and we had a dressing room adjacent to the master bedroom, just crying out to be a nursery. What were we waiting for?

Our third baby was due, with inappropriate vicarage timing, on Christmas Eve, and I was booked in for another home delivery. Michael's father nobly coped alone in his Beverley parish that Christmas, letting my mother-in-law come over to stay in Halifax. No sign of an imminent baby on Christmas Eve, so I went with Michael to join with the nurses who walked from ward to ward singing carols by candlelight. Michael, as chaplain, led the procession, and I walked by his side resplendently pregnant under my red cloak. I am sure many of the patients thought I was padded out, as a visual aid, and were expecting me to bring out a doll from under my cloak as we sang, *Mary had a Baby, Yes Lord*.

I was always aware of the words of the carols and their relationship to the situations in the different parts of the hospital; standing outside sister's office with the telephone ringing out incessantly as relatives rang in their Christmas greetings, we were singing *Ding dong, Merrily on High, in Heaven the Bells are Ringing.*' As old men snored, we sang *Silent Night* and we entered casualty on the words, 'sorrowing, sighing, bleeding, dying ...' Then a more cheerful carol, but this was when my tears started. As I sang 'where a mother laid her baby...' I felt the wait of nine months and the weight of another large baby whom I desperately longed to see and suckle.

I returned to the vicarage feeling cheated that my Christmas baby had not arrived. Michael was in his usual 'I want to go to bed and not stay up for a midnight service' mode. This temporary bad mood always lasted from 8pm to 10pm and it was better to send him upstairs for a sleep before reviving him with a sherry and a mince-pie before he went over to church just before eleven. At five past eleven he was back, in a flap. I could hear him rummaging around in his study. 'What have you lost this time?' I shouted down from the landing, where I was arranging the carrot, mince-pie and glass of wine for Santa, Rudolph and his helpers.

'I've lost Baby Jesus' he replied. This was a change from the usual answer of car keys or diary, and I had to acknowledge that the absence of Jesus on Christmas Eve was something of a calamity.

It was customary for the manger to be set up with Mary, Joseph and shepherds on the Sunday before Christmas, when we had the "Nine Lessons and Carols" service. Then, on Christmas Eve at the beginning of the Midnight service, the choir would process to *It Came upon the Midnight Clear*, halting at the back of the church for the vicar to read the prayer of the blessing of the crib, and to place Baby Jesus gently in the awaiting hay.

Hugging my red cloak over my nightie I plodded over to church to join in the search. Michael was sure he had put Baby Jesus on the ledge in the pulpit. Having convinced myself that he was nowhere in the pulpit, I turned my attention to the adjacent windowsill. There, sleeping in heavenly peace on a bed of prickly holly, was the Christ child, who had been rudely awakened from his pulpit sanctuary by an over zealous cleaner administering an extra Christmas sparkle to the pulpit earlier in the evening. All was now well in church. Not so at the vicarage. The children who had been fast asleep when I left were both wide awake on the landing, looking on in amazement at their grandma astride the rocking horse, which was meant as the Big Surprise. Santa's glass of wine had been drunk. Grandma was looking rosy and was giggling.

Chapter 9

Christmas morning started five hours after Michael had crawled into bed after the midnight service. Christopher was already assembling his new Mousetrap game, Pauline was examining her new doll to see if it had knickers on, and Grandma was making a strong coffee. Our 'Christmas Eve baby' was showing no signs of appearing and was merely continuing to enjoy stretch and kick exercises despite the limitations of the size of its gym. Michael went off to take the 8am Communion and I cooked bacon and eggs which were ready at 8.45am so that he could have a good breakfast before scuttling down the road to start his Communions at the hospital.

It was nearly 9am before I remembered he had said that after the service he would go up the church tower with the lay reader to put up the flag. Recent gales had whipped the rope from its moorings and it would have to be posted through the metal loop at the top of the pole. In readiness for this posting operation he had taken all my vacuum cleaner pipes and those of a neighbour, and lashed them together with my university scarf. His idea was to post the new rope up through the length of tubing and thread it through the flagpole loop.

His bacon was going cold and the egg was hard, so I put his breakfast into the oven, and went to the lounge to look out at the church tower, expecting by now to see the St. George's flag billowing out. What I saw was two men clutching the parapet and laughing hysterically. They still had the flag in their hands, but flying majestically was my green, yellow and blue Nottingham University scarf to the accompaniment of pipes. Vacuum cleaner pipes. Michael left the reader to untangle this problem; he had to rush to hospital and be back in time for the Christmas morning service.

Vicarage children have to be very patient on Christmas Day – waiting for daddy to finish all his services and duties before the present-opening can begin. However we did let them choose three presents to open before Church. So it was that Pauline chose her new doll to sit with her in the pew. I was pleased our youngest was so good on Christmas morning, for she had a reputation as a wanderer – usually up the side aisle so she could get a better look at daddy. Once a church warden had retrieved her and returned her to me in our pew, as he sang loudly 'Perverse and foolish oft she strayed,' and I can never again sing *The King of Love My Shepherd is*, without thinking of Pauline.

Today, however, she was not wandering, but putting her doll to sleep on a bed of hassocks. For a change I could actually concentrate on the service, and rashly closed my eyes for the prayer of consecration. I had therefore no idea that Pauline was by now undressing her doll, and finding a string to pull from the middle of its back. As Michael lifted up the chalice, an automated voice pierced the holy stillness with a loud 'I want a wee-wee'. I wanted to crawl under the pew – not an easy option at nine months and one day of pregnancy.

The congregation was understanding and kind. 'You're still around then,' they said, stating the obvious. Boxing Day was a Sunday and my presence at church elicited the same inane comment. Michael's mother left on the Monday; her replacement was my sister from Devon. She stayed until Friday. I braced myself to go to church again on Sunday January 2nd, but after the third 'what – no baby yet?' I dissolved into tears and went back to the vicarage. There is a limit to how many 'aids to speed up birth' you can take.

Plums were not in season; I did not want to jog round the park, and I had no intention of taking castor oil. It was the ninth day of Christmas and I wanted my true love to give to me a pink cuddly baby, never mind nine ladies dancing.

I felt unusually hungry on the Monday, so cooked a steak and kidney pie for lunch before getting Christopher and Pauline ready to go to the NSPCC party. (No – I wasn't cruel to my children; the party was given annually for children who had donated to the cause by putting pennies into a Blue Egg collecting box). The organiser arrived at the vicarage door at 1.30pm to collect the key for the church hall. I answered. I don't need to spell out her greeting. Before she got onto the castor oil I assured her that as soon as the children had been sent down to the party I would curl up in bed and have the baby while they were out.

I took advantage of a quiet afternoon to have a nap, but around four o'clock I woke up with bad backache. The midwife came at half past, and at 6.15pm a dark haired daughter arrived, with no apologies for being late, and weighing in at nine pounds six ounces. The party organiser rang the vicarage bell at 6.30pm to hand in the keys. Michael answered the door. 'Well, did your wife curl up and have the baby while we were having the party?' she asked, jokingly. 'Yes, it's a girl and we're calling her Rosemary Elizabeth,' he replied. She was starting to laugh at his quick repartee, when Rosemary let out a loud cry, and the midwife came out to retrieve a bag from her car.

And so it was that the first visitor to view our newly born baby was an incredulous lady from the NSPCC.

Both grandmas were soon on the scene, vying with each other for space in the kitchen. Despite its vastness, this Victorian vicarage had a tiny kitchen, once the maid's scullery. The former kitchen had been made into a family living room. My mother was keen on doing the laundry;

Michael's mother's forte was baking. As I lay in state upstairs cooing over my baby, I heard voices getting louder below. My mother brought me a milky coffee and confessed that while still being best friends with Michael's mother, she did find it difficult to get the nappies washed amid so much floury baking. On the other hand Michael's mother confided to him that she couldn't do all the baking she wanted to, because the washing machine was always in the middle of the floor. Notwithstanding all the soapsuds she did manage to produce more cakes and pies than she could find room to store in our cupboards. Her solution was to put the apple pies on the plastic coated racks of what she thought might be a new fangled circular fridge. It was, in fact, a second-hand forerunner of a dishwasher. No good at all for greasy plates, but just about acceptable for the many cup-and-saucer events beloved of vicarages.

Meanwhile my mother was upstairs attending to the many bunches of flowers which the congregation had showered on us. Rosemary demanded lunch. On the midwife's instructions I had expressed some breast milk to give myself some relief on the left side. This procedure is not to be taken on unadvisedly, lightly or wantonly. But painfully and patiently, while sitting in a warm bath. I was thrilled to achieve two fluid ounces into the awaiting Pyrex jug. When I asked my mother where the Pyrex jug was, she assured me she had just washed it up. 'It had some water in, so I topped up the chrysanthemums on the landing.' I tried not to be cross, but it's difficult not to cry, two days after having a baby, and when that baby is crying for the milk that now resides in a crystal vase. I soon bounced back. So did the chrysanthemums. They lasted until my birthday in the middle of February. Would Interflora be interested in a new formula, I wondered?

My mother went downstairs somewhat chastened, to wash up the coffee cups. She hastily put them at the front of the dishwasher and switched on. Aluminium foil plates catapulted their offerings onto the glass front, and apple puree mingled with blue powder and soap suds. Then the eruptions began.

'Fancy putting coffee cups in when you could see there were apple pies there!'

'Fancy putting apple pies in a dishwasher!'

Michael began the task of scraping the soapy pastry from the machine. The grandmas began the task of reconciliation. I began to squeeze droplets of milk into the Pyrex jug, and wickedly shouted downstairs, 'I think the chrysanths are flagging' and 'is there any apple pie for tea?'

The next day the grandmas left.

Chapter 10

Not only did I now have a big house to 'follow' but a busy husband and three young children too. Surely this was enough to excuse me from further involvement with parish activities? Unlike many of my contemporaries, I never mastered the art of saying 'no' when asked if I would do another job. Maybe I should have been firmer. But then I might I have missed out on so many facets of life which I learned to enjoy and which I now treasure.

At the Diocesan Council meeting of the Mothers' Union in Wakefield, the president asked for volunteers to go to Leeds for a three day course on local radio. I looked round the hall and saw rows of ladies with their arms folded, and their eyes resolutely fixed on the floor. The president was looking desperate. Her questioning eyes met mine. I found myself nodding. My fate was sealed.

The next month I was out on the streets of Leeds armed with a portable tape recorder, asking men coming out of the bus depot whether they preferred stockings to tights. We were learning how to assemble vox pops, and this was the question I had pulled out of the hat. Eager to show off that I had mastered the technique of the recorder, and keen to learn how to edit out some of the unsavoury language that had ensued, I dashed back to the conference room and played back my tape. Then, and only then, did I realise that it had not been a good idea to conduct my vox pop right next to a pelican crossing and its intrusive bleeps. So I had to go out and do it all over again, with a new question to ask: 'What do the letters MU stand for?' I had hitherto taken it for granted that everyone would know it stood for

Mothers' Union. Not so. To most of the men it stood for Miners' Union or Manchester United. I had much to learn.

Other parts of the local radio course included being interviewed and sharing a group discussion. I did not excel in these. However my confidence rose when it came to interviewing others, probably because I had done plenty of this in my medical social work days. At the end of the three days we received a written school-type report, in which I gained my highest mark, an A-, for 'writing for radio'. Flushed with this success I returned home feeling I was the North of England's answer to *Thought for the Day*. I sent off several scripts to BBC Radio Leeds and heard nothing. On enquiry I learned that they had not liked them. I tried again, with a different style. They were not accepted. I needed to learn technique, so I paid to go on a 'Writing for Radio' course at Bushey, near Watford. I rang up BBC Radio Leeds to tell them that my report said I had promise, but before I could get a word in, the religious programmes chief asked if I would be willing to take over the Halifax and Huddersfield area as a roving reporter for the weekly "God slot".

I was loaned a Uher tape recorder and given a crash course on doing my own splicing, with a razor blade and sticky tape. Rosemary, four, was about to start school, so I thought I would have plenty of extra time for this new pursuit. I certainly needed it. When told I should aim at producing four minutes of broadcast material each week, I had visions of one, or at the most two hours of work. I had not taken into account my thinking time; what was in the news? Who, of note, was coming to the area this week? Not all my interviewees were willing to come to our house to be interviewed, so I had to allow travelling time to go to them. Not everyone was a seasoned broadcaster; some needed several tries before they felt confident. One of my first outings was to interview a young Roman Catholic priest about Anglican/RC relations.

I was nervous, but tried not to show it. He was nervous and did show it. We had several dummy runs, then went for real. Just as he was getting more fluent and reducing the number of er – ers I would have to edit out, there was a roaring sound outside the study door. His housekeeper had started up the Hoover. She was re-routed to the bedroom and we started again. This time the interruption came from the priest's large black Labrador who howled outside the door. 'It would be better to let him in,' said the priest. The beast entered and stretched out between us. The interview went splendidly and I played it back to reassure my nervous interviewee. Horror of horrors - the background noise was one of very heavy breathing. The microphone had picked up every breath of the somnolent dog. The message to the listener would certainly have been one of very cordial Anglican/RC relations! Third time lucky, I prayed, as we went over the questions and answers yet again. I had counted my chickens too soon. I had yet to learn that it was wise to stop all clocks – especially those that chimed in with jolly Westminster tunes on the quarter hour.

Once I was home I discovered that splicing had as many hazards as doing the recording. One premature cut of the razor blade and the wrong word had been edited out. One phone call in the middle of rearranging cut-up pieces of tape hanging on a line, suspended with clothes pegs, and I would end up with a load of non-sequiturs or gibberish. When I had successfully spliced the tape, written my lead-in, and popped the whole thing in the post I wallowed in a feeling of euphoria. The following Friday at noon I demanded complete silence as I listened to my four minute "baby" which had had a gestation period of several hours. 'Do I really have such a pronounced Yorkshire accent?' I asked, before I went off in search of inspiration for next week's interview, and to practise my vowel sounds.

In contrast to the nervous RC priest, I had the good fortune to interview some eminent authors and churchmen who were well used to the recording procedure, and who fed me with the questions they wanted me to ask. Best of all was Bishop Stephen Neill who had done an interview on his latest book for Radio Four earlier in the day, and nodded his head obligingly to cue me in for my next question. I returned home jubilant with no editing required of me; just the lead in to write. Sometimes this job could be a doddle!

Not every week brought forth newsworthy people or events, so I was encouraged to build up a store of timeless recordings for use in the lean weeks. Children were naturals at the microphone, so I interviewed Pauline's junior school friends on what they thought of Church services ("boring") and captured Rosemary's thoughts on her infants' nativity play: 'I don't think Mary was very kind. She didn't give Jesus any blankets. I think the straw went up his bottom.'

I even recorded our black Labrador. He had two pet hates. One was the sound of church bells and the other was church music – particularly psalm chants. I tuned in most days to the daily service on the radio, only to have my devotions interrupted by the dog who would throw back his head and howl like a wolf throughout the psalm. When he heard himself played back on BBC Radio Leeds he was terrified, and ran to cower under the sideboard.

During my seven years of working for BBC Radio Leeds I didn't accrue a fortune. The work was unpaid, though I was given a mug and a T-shirt, and a one-off honorarium of £10 to cover travel expenses. However I did enjoy the opportunities to meet so many interesting and kind people, with wonderful stories to tell – like the young man who was on furlough from Nepal where he had gone out with the Church Missionary Society. He was alight with passion for his job, but the thing that enthralled me most, and the only thing I can now remember, was his enthusiasm for his scheme for making methane gas from cow dung. Thanks to the Mothers' Union president for volunteering me, way back in 1976, I was now in the forefront of research into alternatives to fossil fuel in the Himalayas.

1976 was the centenary of the Mothers' Union, founded by another vicar's wife, Mary Sumner, in Old Alresford in the Winchester Diocese. Our Halifax deanery decided to celebrate this with a pageant in Halifax parish church, an ancient and large church which had once vied with Wakefield to become the cathedral. Somehow I was volunteered to co-write the script, *Mothers' Union past, present and future*. Each of the seventeen branches was allocated a part, and as I possessed a family heirloom Victorian christening gown, I gave my branch the part that included the baptism of Mary Sumner's first baby. A suitably large doll was loaned with the instructions that we were to treat her gently as she was very old. She had flexible limbs, joined to the body with hooks and rubber bands. Unfortunately the head was attached in a similar way, and at the crucial moment in the pageant, the vicar of Halifax was a bit heavy handed in signing the cross on her forehead. The rubber band snapped and Mary Sumner watched in horror as her baby's head rolled down the main aisle. The solemnity of the occasion and the next piece of narration were drowned in the giggles of the thousand-strong congregation. I gazed at the pink disembodied head with horror, and reflected that this church was dedicated to John the Baptist. Surely he would understand.

The pageant reached its climax with a procession of the entire cast, and headless baby, to the strains of a special hymn I had written – *O God of All That has Been*. I stood by the font at the West end of the church with an overwhelming and tear-jerking feeling of fulfilment. The following week my head grew bigger as I basked in the compliments of many people over the success of the pageant. Some younger women had even asked to join the Mothers' Union as a result of watching it. I should have known that pride went before a fall. Some days later at a Mothers' Union deanery coffee morning a lady from the neighbouring parish of All Saints came over to me and said, 'Mrs Walker, congratulations on that wonderful pageant.' I glowed. But then she added, 'the only thing that spoiled it was that terrible hymn at the end. Who on earth wrote that?' I am afraid I was a coward. I stuttered something like, 'I – er – I don't know. I'll find out.' Well, she would have been so embarrassed if I'd told her it was me, wouldn't she? I was only telling a white lie in order to spare her.

The only trouble was that for my remaining years in Halifax I had to cross over the road every time I saw her approaching, so fearful was I that she would ask me if I'd found out the unfortunate author of "that terrible hymn".

It was in 1986, when we had moved to our next parish, that I received a letter from the Halifax deanery saying they hoped to stage the pageant again, and asking if they could have permission to include my hymn?

I readily gave permission, with one proviso. They must not put on the service sheet, "written by Margaret Walker". If anyone asked who wrote that awful hymn they were to answer, 'I'll find out'.

Chapter 11

The year of the Mothers' Union Pageant, 1976 was the year of the drought. Even in the Pennines, where rain was usually frequent, we had standpipes at the ready. The vicarage may have been a big house to follow, but that summer it came into its own as the second coolest house in the parish. Visitors seemed loath to leave our airy rooms, and I do believe the summer congregations burgeoned. It was cool to go to Church!

We had always had our Mothers' Union outings in June. They had invariably been wet. This year we voted to try September, for we all knew that the week the schools went back after the long holiday was the week the sun always shone. Having suffered many meetings, when thrashing out the venue for the summer trip took as long as the talk, I had craftily suggested a "Mystery Trip". Nobody could argue about the venue this year. I was equally determined not to have arguments about the catering. Last year, when a plate of attractively arranged salmon came into view, Mrs Hepplethwaite had sworn to God that she had ordered fish, even though my check list distinctly bore "Mixed Grill" next to her name. I had been looking forward to eating the salmon I had ordered and I found it very hard to do the Christian thing. I eyed Mrs Hepplethwaite's succulent fish with envy as I swapped plates, cut into a grisly sausage and scooped up the black pudding in a serviette to give to the dog.

1976. The outing with a difference. A September Mystery Trip, when all members were to be issued with a laminated card bearing the menu they had chosen – in their own hand-writing. The first Thursday in June, when we would normally have had our outing, was very hot. We held our meeting in a small, low-ceilinged room in the church hall, and I'm afraid that several elderly members nodded off in the heat.

'Wouldn't it have been lovely for our outing!' they said. The first Thursday in July was even hotter. We sizzled through August. By September we were all desperate to get out of the town. I knew they would love the mystery venue up in the Dales.

We had been in the coach for ten minutes when there was a flash of lightning and a terrific roar of thunder. Three months worth of rain fell out of the sky on the first Thursday of September. Nobody had brought a raincoat or umbrella. Water ran through our sandals as we sloshed across the car park at Skipton. At least we had the meal to look forward to. I had ordered salmon. It said so in my handwriting on my laminated card. The waiter changed my knife and fork for a fish knife and fish fork. Things were looking good. It was then I saw Mrs Sutcliffe approaching, and I knew my salmon was in jeopardy.

'Mrs Walker, I'm ever so sorry, but I see that I ordered ham, egg and chips, and now the Doctor has put me on a fat free diet on account of my gallstones. You don't think anyone would swap me her salmon salad, do you?

I should have said 'no', but old Mrs Sutcliffe had so looked forward to this day out. Her peaky face and bedraggled wet hair added pathos to the scene. I submissively handed over my fish knife and fork and prayed that my gall bladder would cope with the fatty exchange offering, and that my Christian charity would cope with the gathering storm of mutterings; 'we should never have changed the date of the outing to September.'

I was always wary of mutterings. An acute sense of hearing is not always an asset, as I could often tune into the whispered conversations going on in the pew behind when the unsuspecting complainants were launching into a moan about the coldness of the church, the behaviour of the Sunday school, or how they didn't like people wandering around giving "The Peace". I was even more wary of people who prefaced their conversation with, 'Can I have a word?' This, being interpreted, usually meant 'will you tell the vicar that I am upset about...'. I would try to listen despite the throbbing of my heart and the rising of my hackles that people should think they had carte blanche to criticise my husband. If I had a dispute with the bank manager I would never have dreamed of discussing it with the bank manager's wife first. And if the milk on the doorstep had gone off I would not have laid into the milkman's wife.

So, having listened to a tirade about rabbits eating the flowers on the graves, or the distress of Mrs Jones because the vicar hadn't shaken her hand last Sunday, but had seemed preoccupied with talking to a wedding couple, I would filter out what I would pass on. If I felt it would be helpful I would broach the subject with Michael later in the week - never on a Sunday. Other things, like Mary, I kept in my heart and pondered them, usually in the early hours of the morning, when problems always loom larger than is their wont.

One day in 1978, Angela, our youngest lay reader, fresh from Durham University, called me aside after Matins, and said, 'Margaret, can I have a word?' My heart plummeted, but it need not have done. She was animated and persuasive as she propounded her idea of forming a dance-drama group in the church, as an aid to worship. As I was musical, would I be prepared to help? Of course I would. She would gather together some dancers and narrators and we would meet next month on a Sunday afternoon in the church hall.

I could sense her disappointment when, of the seven people who had turned up, three were willing to be narrators, one would help with choreography, one (me) would help with the music, but only two would do the dance/drama. We went away to try to recruit more support by the next Sunday. A husband of one of the dance volunteers said he would do the music, which meant I had no excuse not to become a dancer. My daughter, Rosemary, was six and maybe thought she would appear in a tutu when I asked if she would like to be in the dance team. Our first production, based on the creation story, lasted almost an hour and our premiere was performed in the nearby United Reformed Church where we had a carpeted floor and could dance 'in the round'.

The congregation seemed genuinely moved at the Bible being brought to life through music, mime, dance, narration and meditation. We, who had danced, were also deeply touched. Only one man came up to us after the service to say how shocked he was to see grown women in black leotards and tights prancing around a sacred place. He was a retired priest, of the old school, and could not reconcile what we were doing with a gospel presentation. However, we took his words to heart, and went to the market to buy yards of blue satin, with which to make semi-circular wrap-over skirts to cover our thighs. Extra ones were used to form cloaks or veils when appropriate.

Whether it was the success of our first presentation or the fact that we now had skirts, I know not, but we had a surge of enthusiasm for our dance-drama team, which at its height included 25 participants. Alma, our choreographer had the gift of matching music to the theme, and then adding movements to the rhythm and feeling of the melody. The role I enjoyed most was in the *Prodigal Son* sequence, danced to Rimsky-Korsakov's *Sheherazade*. I wore a red satin skirt, as leader of the wayward women, with whom the Prodigal became acquainted after he had taken his inheritance. To this day Michael is embarrassed if this piece of music comes on the radio while a visitor is in the house, as I cannot help but get up and do a hip wiggling, provocative dance sequence, flashing my eyes and beckoning any unwary males around me. Similarly, when the theme music from *The Onedin Line* is played, I am likely to kneel down and waft my arms around, in an attempt to look like a crashing wave, which was my part in the sequence of *Paul's shipwreck*.

The pinnacle of our time in the dance-drama team was performing in the cathedral at a special service for those with hearing and speech difficulties. We were to dance an extract from our sequence on death and resurrection. Dressed in black leotards, with our leader as a skeleton, bones depicted in luminous paint, we sat in the Lady Chapel awaiting our slot in the service. During the signed hymn prior to our dance, our leader made the mistake of standing up and turning round to face the congregation. As she rose from behind a substantial tomb and the light above picked out her luminosity, I was aware of the people on the front row of the congregation looking around for a hasty exit!

Sometimes we danced, not so much for others, as for ourselves. One Lent we ran a "keep fit, in body, mind and spirit" session on Sunday afternoons. Here we exercised our body to music, then had a short Bible reading and study, followed by relaxation and meditation, and of course, a cup of tea. These sessions attracted other people, knowing they hadn't to perform in front of a congregation and we even had men!

In contrast to our religious dance-drama we also performed at parish social occasions. Most memorable was a Church Fellowship Christmas party where we did the cancan. We had to get really fit for such exuberant leg kicks, and were careful to do our warm-ups to prevent muscle strain. Extravagant costumes with feathers and froufrou were hired from the local theatre, and we put on our bright red lipstick and rouge with Parisian abandon. Our performance was greeted with cheers and foot stamping and cries of 'encore'. Offenbach would have been proud. He might also have been amused that in our chorus line up were the organist's wife and three vicars' wives.

However, there was one person who was definitely not amused. I was taken aside immediately by a gentleman who "wanted a word". He had been shocked to see such a performance at a Church event, and even more shocked that I had been a participant. He would never come to a Church social event again. It had been bad enough seeing our black tights and leotards in our first religious dance-drama, but to see us dance the cancan in a church hall was "the end". I was sorry he saw it this way. For me, the purchase of black fishnet tights was just the beginning.

Chapter 12

The black fishnets languished for a while in my drawer awaiting another excuse for an outing – possibly in conjunction with my tap shoes, for my excursion into religious dance-drama and the cancan led me onto folk dancing, circle dancing and tap. But in the late 1970s it was my ordinary black stockings that came out of the drawer. In the space of three years my father, my brother and my mother had died, and I was left feeling unusually depressed.

At Christmas everyone seemed to be having family to stay. I felt suddenly bereft, and one night gave way to self-pitying tears. Michael tried to comfort me, by pointing out, quite rightly, that we were so blessed in that we had each other and three lovely children, while many people would be spending Christmas entirely alone, and would maybe see nobody over the whole Christmas period. A good cry and a sleep later and perspective became gradually restored. With it came the thought that we could invite to the vicarage for a Christmas meal, those who would otherwise be alone. Christmas Day was not ideal, as we had morning services and always went round the hospital wards on Christmas afternoon to talk to patients who had no visitors. Our children enjoyed seeing all the wonderful decorations in the infirmary, and helped to eat up some of the excess chocolates and cakes which abounded in every ward. How about Boxing Day? This seemed a good day for our meal, which we came to call "our lonely lunch".

We let it be made known that anyone who lived alone and who would like to come to lunch, would be welcome at the vicarage at 12 noon, and we would arrange transport. As the invitation was open until the very last minute we had no idea how many to cater for. In the event we had twelve for our first "lonely lunch". We opened up our large dining room and lounge into one long room, and gave the electric storage heaters a rare warming up to their top temperature. Together with a coal fire and a gas fire we managed to reach the dizzy heights of 63°F. Those who had not been able to get to church on Christmas Day and who were prepared to descend into lower temperatures went into the study for a short service. Meanwhile other guests sat around the table while "Wellybob Sam" entertained them on the piano. He was rather unusually attired for a pianist, in his tweed jacket worn over a bare chest, and his trousers tucked into black wellies. His carroty hair did not have its customary flat cap to hold it down, so it stuck out like porcupine quills. Sam had no fixed abode, but enjoyed his cheese sandwich and mug of tea every Sunday morning in the vicarage porch. Until he made his debut that first Christmas we had no idea of his musical talent. He glowed with self-worth at the subsequent applause, and then sat down next to one of the wealthier widows of the parish, whose neck was swathed in pearls, and whose wrinkled fingers clanked with rings. She had a large house, and plenty of money, but no-one to assuage her seasonal loneliness. Now she had Sam next to her, and they were soon in an animated conversation about Mozart.

The menu was simple, that first year - soup, pork pie and salad, trifle, coffee and mince pies. Afterwards we sang carols around the fire until half past three when we started to ferry our guests home. By the comments we received we knew that this lunch could not be a one-off event. The next Christmas some of our parishioners offered to help. One family came early and helped set the tables, another took up their place in the kitchen for washing-up duties, while others waited on table, and my friend Alma, from the dance-drama group, and I did an after-meal cabaret act. After our rendition of Eartha Kitt's *I'm Just an Old Fashioned Girl*, our younger daughter Rosemary, and her friend Katharine enchanted everyone with *Me and My Teddy Bear*. Our guests went home full of good cheer and full of "special" turkey. A local farmer had heard about our lunch, and offered me his "special" turkeys. I had no idea what to expect, but they were birds with plenty of meat on, albeit with legs that must have been knocked awry in the packing machine. Each year I took up the challenge to cook the turkey meat in a different way – in wine, with mushrooms and with different stuffing.

The pudding course had grown from just trifle to a choice of Christmas pudding or trifle, thanks to the offers of kind parishioners. Marguerite had promised to provide two large trifles, which would be delivered to the vicarage on Boxing Day morning. In the rush to set tables, prepare the turkey, and then start greeting the guests I had failed to observe that no trifles had appeared. However we coped admirably when dessert time came, by opening tins of fruit salad and ferrying in ice cream from a neighbour's freezer. We didn't even have a fridge at the time; the normal temperature of the vicarage sufficed! It was while we were singing carols afterwards that the mystery of the missing trifles was solved. Our black Labrador, Pinza regurgitated them onto the hearth rug in front of all our visitors. Marguerite had misguidedly left them on the back doorstep, convinced that someone would find them. Unfortunately it was Pinza who had eaten the contents of the two huge bowls, and who had literally bitten off more than he could chew.

One lady who longed to come to our lunch was Miss Johnson, but she was not eligible for the first two years as she had an ex-missionary sister staying with her. When the sister died, Miss Johnson was quick off the mark to register her wish to be put on our lunch list. She was in her nineties, lived in a flat at the top of a long flight of steps, and often turned up at church an hour or two too early for evensong so she would be invited over to the vicarage for tea. Miss Johnson had served as a cook for a titled family, and was most appreciative of my lacy cloth and ivy leaf china tea service. It was high praise when she said to me, 'Mrs Walker, you do boil a very nice egg.' Now it was my turn to show that I could cook a very nice turkey.

Next Boxing Day, a black Bentley, driven by one of our parishioners, collected Miss Johnson, neatly dressed in a black dress and coat, and Mother Riley-type hat. At table she sat next to Mr Hepplethwaite, a tall, gaunt man with thick-rimmed spectacles, who frightened us all by a huge choking fit in the middle of the main course. Miss Gardener, a timid middle-aged lady showed great presence of mind and thumped Mr Hepplethwaite firmly between his shoulder blades. Out shot the offending morsel, together with his top set of false teeth, which landed in the middle of the salad bowl. Unperturbed, he reached out for them, and stuffed them and a lettuce leaf into his mouth and continued devouring his turkey.

After the carols and cabaret Miss Johnson came up to me and complimented me on the "delicious meal". My head swelled visibly, but soon shrank back to size as I heard her parting shot to Michael – 'Next year, please tell your wife to have the plates hotter.'

I had no hostess trolley and despite a large vicarage I had a miniscule kitchen. By now we had 31 guests on our list, so heating up the plates was not easy. The following year I instructed the kitchen staff to plunge all the dinner plates into near-boiling water. All went well, and that night Michael and I snuggled into bed, reviewing yet another successful "lonely lunch".

'At least the plates were hot,' I said. 'Miss Johnson didn't complain this year.'

'Margaret, I don't remember seeing Miss Johnson,' was Michael's disconcerting reply. We went round the table, recalling who had sat where. Miss Johnson was not on our mental map. Miss Johnston, with a 't', was. Truth dawned when I consulted my transport list. A newcomer to the parish had volunteered as a chauffeur and had misguidedly gone to the wrong house. When Miss Johnston had answered the door and found a handsome man with a Mercedes wanting to take her to the vicarage, she had not needed to be asked twice, even though she lived with two sisters and was therefore not eligible for the lunch.

We thought of poor Miss Johnson, who would have been sitting waiting in her black coat and hat, waiting for the chauffeur who never turned up. What could we do? At ten minutes past midnight, nothing. Michael volunteered to go round to Miss Johnson the next morning and take her some turkey, a few mince pies and a little gift, along with profuse apologies for the mix-up.

Climbing up the narrow steps to her flat he rang the bell. Before he could utter a word, Miss Johnson greeted him with 'Oh vicar, what a lovely lunch we had yesterday. Do you know, I must have been so tired when I returned home that I nodded off to sleep in my chair with my hat and coat still on. When I woke up the fire was nearly out.' Somewhat bemused, Michael decided not to apologise, but just to say that he had brought round some more of that nice turkey, and that he was so glad she had enjoyed the party.

On his return we pondered over this strange happening, and could only conclude that she had been sitting in her chair by the fire, hat and coat on, waiting for the driver, and had nodded off to sleep. In her dreams she had thought she was at the vicarage enjoying the lunch. As Michael reminded me, 'God moves in a mysterious way, his wonders to perform.' He had certainly done it on that Boxing Day afternoon.

Miss Johnson didn't live to see the next "lonely lunch", but as we said Grace we thought of her, and prayed that the plates would be hot in heaven.

Chapter 13

Christmas gave way to Epiphany, and before the last pine needles had been unthreaded from the Crossley's Criterion cord carpet, we were into the purple of Lent, and I was drawing up the list for ordering Easter lilies "in memoriam".

It never ceased to amaze me that the flower list could be vacant for many weeks, but that at Easter people were prepared to pay large sums of money for lilies, and this list was always oversubscribed. I had never liked lilies, and liked them even less after getting to know their malevolent whims. If Easter was late we risked having flowers that bruised and went brown before Low Sunday. If Easter was early the flowers would arrive in tight bud, and in order to have some white showing on Easter Day I had to whisk them in and out of various rooms to catch the moving sunshine, and sometimes I even resorted to blowing them with a hair drier. I learned to touch these dreaded blooms with deference if my hands and clothes were to stay unstained by the penetrating dye from the pollen.

No sooner had the last falling lily petals been scooped up from the sanctuary floor than Ascension Day approached. My children went to the local church school, and after the Ascension morning service they had a holiday. I didn't. Most of my children's friends' mums went out to work, so on this day we always had friends to stay. We may not have had much money, but we did have a large house whose two staircases and five attics made hide and seek, and games of sardines, attractive options. 'My dad will take you up the church tower' was the children's annual Ascension-tide offer. I declined to go with them, not even daring to look up to see them lolling on the parapets. Nowadays Health and Safety would demand risk assessments, and as for Child Protection laws…!

Whitsuntide followed red and hot on the heels of Ascension. We didn't have a television, but I did not need a weather forecaster to predict that we would soon be in for a wild and windy period which would be guaranteed to dash the peonies against the wall and shed their Whitsuntide blooms across the lawn, rather than radiating from the polished vases on the altar. Don't tell it abroad, but I have been known to supplement the few remaining peonies with some Remembrance poppies skilfully wired around the background greenery.

On the second Saturday in June there was another festival. This was the annual Halifax Charity Gala (pronounced gay-la, and never gar-la). Huge numbers of floats would process from the bottom of town up the hills to Manor Heath Park where there would be stalls, competitions, and all the fun of the fair to tempt people to part with their money "in a good cause".

Michael was chairman of the Children's Society, so I usually dressed up in some outrageous costume and walked beside their float collecting money on the procession route. Out came the black fishnets and, once, when I had hoped the sun would shine, out came the bikini and grass skirt. When the float theme was the Pied Piper of Hamelin the committee found a small rat's costume for Rosemary, aged two. I was to push her thus dressed, in her pushchair, and it was deemed that I too should dress as a rat. Unfortunately the only costume available was for that of a 10-year-old. I know I was only a size 10, but it was a tight squeeze. When I stood erect to look at the result in the mirror I realised there was a big difference between the anatomy of a 10-year-old and a 33-year-old. The front fastening was press-studs, which went pop, pop, pop all the way down, revealing more than befitted a vicar's wife. Hence I did the two-mile walk up to the park in a stooping posture. The fancy dress judges thought I was the Hunchback of Notre Dame. I didn't collect much money, as I couldn't even lift my face high enough to give eye contact to the crowds, which lined the pavements en route. However my little rat fell asleep on the way, and well-wishers threw their coppers into the seaside bucket which dangled from her pushchair, amid sympathetic oohs and aahs, and between us we collected a goodly amount.

The older children went into the fancy dress competition. Pauline and her friend Lorraine went dressed as lilac fairies, which tells you a lot about the climate up in the Pennines. Christopher opted for "The Most Original" fancy dress category, dressed as a chef on roller skates and with a paper plate full of salad sewn onto the top of the chef's hat; he entered as "Meal on Wheels"'. It was unfortunate that a new category had been created that year – the Best Fancy Dress on Horseback. All my culinary arrangement and painstaking pushing of needle and cotton through paper plate and starched hat were suddenly to no avail, as a frisky pony saw his chance of a lunchtime feast. They say there's no such thing as a free meal. Don't you believe it!

As a vicar's wife I had become proficient in the folding of raffle tickets, and as a speaker at WI meetings I had passed my proficiency badge in judging "Best Dressed Clothes Pegs", Victoria sandwich cakes and dried flower arrangements. Now a new challenge awaited me – I was to be a judge at the Gala Baby Show. As the other two judges and I walked over to the large tent we were greeted by much wailing, and by angry young mothers who were quite rightly incensed by the crashing of a tent pole narrowly missing their offspring. It was a hot and sultry day, and we felt that a very quick viewing of the babies was the best option. Armed with clipboards and papers numbered 1 to 102, we patrolled the mums and babies. The organiser had misguidedly stuck raffle ticket numbers on the babies, rather than give them to the mothers to hold. It soon became obvious that this was a very bad idea; in many cases the babies had plucked off their numbers and stuffed them into their mouths, producing pink, green and blue saliva down their white dresses and romper suits.

We judges did our best, though I can't think how we came to a unanimous decision. The whole thing was a nightmare. Only three mothers came to shake hands with us. The other ninety-nine threw malicious looks in our direction. I realised I had lost the goodwill of most of our Sunday school parents, and any hope of forming a Young Wives' group had been dashed. I turned my attention to the Darby and Joan club who met in our church hall the following Wednesday. One grandma arrived at the meeting pushing a pram. 'What a lovely baby', I cooed. 'A pity you didn't think so last Saturday,' came the reply.

The following year I had a phone call from the Gala organiser asking if I would judge the baby competition again. Thinking quickly I said I was awfully sorry, but I was an essential part of the Children's Society float. It was a white lie at the time, which I partly redeemed by begging my husband to let me dress as a dormouse on their Alice in Wonderland float. The committee agreed and I rejoiced. That was until I saw my costume. It looked familiar, and I noticed the press-studs were pulling away from the rat grey material. I decided there and then to find another escape route to the baby competition judging. I would enter the adult fancy dress competition, and dress as a devil. Out came the black leotard and black calf boots. Now where did I put my black fishnet tights?

Chapter 14

It is easy to look back and remember the good times, the happy times and the fun times. Maybe memory prefers to push the sad and hurtful events into the recesses of our mind. Yet if I push my memory stick into the past I can and do retrieve them.

There were times when I ran into my secret sanctuary to let the welling tears overflow, then to wipe my eyes and blow my nose on the toilet paper, and emerge to face the demands of the parish. The vicar's wife is so often used as a go-between, and such a position is not always to be relished. What always infuriated me were the words, 'So, you're going on holiday again are you?' Yes, we did take our statutory three Sundays off, and of course we always went away, otherwise the telephone and door calls would have continued and Michael would have been expected to take any funeral that cropped up. The people who most seemed to resent our going away were those who left work at 4pm on a Friday and who didn't reappear at their workplace until 9am on a Monday. If we were lucky we managed one whole day off each week, but if it happened to be a weekday we couldn't go far because the children were at school. We tried to take Saturday off so that we could do something as a family, but of course Saturday is the usual day for weddings and for garden fêtes and church bazaars, so our family days out together were limited, and we therefore tried to remedy this by ensuring three full weeks of uninterrupted family holidays.

I was not alone in my toilet weeping. Other vicar's wives had similar gripes, which we saved up to share with one another at the monthly Clergy Wives meetings. Here we could really let our hair down and share with one another things we could never have shared with friends from the parish. After a particularly busy spell, when all my efforts at writing prayers and choosing meaningful hymns had been interrupted endlessly by people on the phone or at the door wanting a word with the vicar, I poured out my frustrations to an older and more experienced vicar's wife. She asked me what these callers at the door had wanted, and then wanted to know how I had responded. Even as I spoke I recalled those words of advice I had been given earlier in my life - 'Margaret, you must learn that your ministry may be a ministry of interruptions'. I needed to remind myself yet again that these people's needs were far more important than the finely-tuned prayers or meaningful hymns on which I had laid such priority. This advice I subsequently passed on to clergy wives and to young curates. It helped me greatly through the remaining years of parish life, and it still does. In concentrating my energy into really listening and responding to another person I was giving them their worth, and possibly giving them the thing that they were craving – a sincere and sympathetic ear, and often a shoulder on which they could cry.

One chapter of our time in Halifax was particularly grim. Returning from a neighbouring church where Michael had been taking a morning Communion, we saw on the side of the parkland, known locally as the Moor, a blue plastic cordon around a solitary shoe, surrounded by many police. We switched on BBC Radio Leeds and learned that the Yorkshire Ripper had struck again. This time it was within yards of the vicarage, and the victim was a young girl from our parish. Her brother had been on our choir. There followed a harrowing time for her family, her neighbours, for our parishioners and for the police. The whole town plunged into anxiety and depression. Children had to be escorted even from the church to the church hall, which was on the same campus. Ladies found walking alone after 8pm were advised by the police to return home. Numbers at evensong dropped dramatically, and our newly formed evening Mothers' Union branch shrivelled while still in embryo.

Some women, worried that they may be seen entering the police caravan, asked if they could speak privately to the police in our vicarage. It was amazing how many of them had a terrifying suspicion that their husband, who had been away from home that fateful night, could have been the Ripper. We had to cope with the ever-inquisitive press, while we were making arrangements for the victim's memorial service. Michael's sermon had to be issued to the police officers who mingled in mufti with the congregation, casting their eagle-eyes along the pews to observe any tell-tale signs when certain key sentences were read. Apparently the perpetrators of such crimes sometimes return in a sadistic desire to see the suffering they have caused.

It was a tense time for everyone, and I can remember the overwhelming feeling of relief when I heard on the radio that the Ripper had been caught. That night I slept less fitfully.

Evensong never made a full recovery, and for many weeks we continued to escort our children down the shadowy path between the vicarage and the church hall. The Ripper incident became a watershed between the old regime and the new. Days of children playing out in the street in the early evening were over. The move towards the more introverted family lifestyle was beginning, accelerated by the increasing popularity of television, and later in the century, the advent of the home computer.

We didn't own a television when the children were small. They are quick to remind us of this fact, and also of the mortification of having to queue up for the free school dinner tickets, when we were on Family Income Supplement. We were grateful for the good quality jumble sales for which our parish was well-known. Here we could rejoice in the early pickings of dresses, hats and suits, as we unpacked the offerings our parishioners had laid on the vicarage doorstep in readiness for the next sale.

Jumble sales were fun. It brought us together as we undid bags, sorted and priced. I learned early on to investigate the pockets of all garments. Sometimes they would reveal coins or redeemable handkerchiefs; on one occasion I found a bacon sandwich of some two or three months vintage. Once, on delving down into a box of what seemed to be musty newspapers I was rewarded with a cache of postcards dating from the First World War, which were subsequently sold at a specialist fair for several pounds.

Two hours before the jumble sales were to start, a queue would begin to form from the hall, down the drive and around the church railings. Inside we started to prepare for the siege. We took out light bulbs and toilet rolls; we had learned that these were easy pickings for our clientele. We then ensured that we had enough helpers to be within touching distance of each other behind the trestle tables. Only then had we any chance of keeping our profit margins high. Large-bosomed matrons would push into our trestles, and while we were recovering our poise, they would fill their bin liners with blouses and skirts and bras from the front of the tables, and drop them to waiting scrawny children who beetled underneath the trestles and out through the emergency exit doors. Here lurked their fathers whose role was to ferry the ill-gotten gains to their dented, clapped-out cars. Each sale we pitted our wits against theirs. I have a feeling they usually won!

Nevertheless, I looked forward to jumble sales, and one autumn I was most upset when the doctor declared me unfit to attend. I had a bad bout of tonsillitis, and was feeling very fragile. On the Monday my friend Alma from the dance-drama group nobly volunteered to do the weekly family wash. Michael turned out the grubby conglomeration of vests, socks, bras, towels, shirts and pants, and bundled them into our dirty sheets. We had hoped to have some clean clothes by Thursday, but none had been returned. That evening the Mothers' Union had a bumper jumble sale, and I felt rather annoyed that they had done so well without me.

The next morning we had a crisis. Nobody had clean socks or pants. Michael was thus encouraged to ring up Alma to ask, without appearing too demanding, when he could call round for the clean washing. 'I did it straight away', she replied. 'I didn't want to disturb Margaret, so I left it in a bin liner in the vicarage porch.' It was then that I realised why the Mothers' Union had had such a good sale. All the jumble donors had left their offerings in black bin liners in the vicarage porch too. All my family's socks, bras, pants, vests and towels, not to mention a Brownie uniform and several sheets had been sold to the highest bidders at the bumper sale. Still convalescent, I cried. Michael laughed. 'What do you want me to do? Ask in the church notices on Sunday who is a 34B and is wearing your bra?' I need not have worried. When this story became known there was an unleashing of such generosity that I cried again. Parcels of replacement clothes appeared at the vicarage, although this time they were not left in bin liners. People gave me money and vouchers, and one good lady gave me her collection of new underwear which she had in a drawer in readiness for the Third World War. I can't think why she wanted to be thus equipped, or whether she would have had time to put it on in the face of a nuclear attack, but I was nonetheless grateful.

By the end of that month I was the best under-weared vicar's wife in the entire province of York. And there wasn't a pair of black fishnet tights in sight!

Chapter 15

Warm underwear was a prerequisite for survival in our Victorian vicarage exposed to the Pennine winds. Downstairs we had electric storage heaters in some rooms, with a mixture of open fires, coke stoves and gas fires. Upstairs we had no heating and no double-glazing. We frequently awoke in winter to find ice on the inside of the windows.

One night, on our return from a parish function, we were told by Tricia, our baby-sitter, that she had wrapped our three-year-old in sheets of newspaper when putting her to bed as she feared that Rosemary would otherwise suffer from hypothermia! In fact we stayed remarkably healthy during our 14 years in this vicarage. Bacteria didn't stand a chance of multiplying in such temperatures.

Sometimes I did yearn for warmth. In a particularly icy winter our pipes froze and we had to trudge through the snow to the church hall to carry buckets of water up to the vicarage, and rely on neighbours for a bath. Global warming hadn't reared its head, and I remember cars being buried on the moor, and Michael dressed in a green Eskimo jacket hacking ice-blocks in the garden to build a wonderful igloo in which our children and their friends played for many weeks. The Diocese had decreed that eventually they would put central heating in our house, but not until there was an interregnum. In other words, however long we stayed we were not going to be the recipients. That was the theory. The practice turned out differently, and all thanks to the bishop who came for confirmation.

Confirmations always filled me with trepidation. After my early days when Christopher had dyed the veils green I had tried to redeem my name. I tried to approach confirmations in an organised fashion, drawing up full lists of the candidates' names, addresses, places of baptism and so on, which I would write up in my best calligraphic style in the registers. I would ensure the veils were pristine and I was always in the church hall in good time on the day to supply hairgrips and safety pins and line up the candidates in the correct order before escorting them into church.

On our first confirmation in Halifax I had the candidates seated by 6.20pm but was alarmed that there was no sign of either Michael or the bishop. I dashed over to the vicarage. They were not having a preparatory prayer in the study. No, they were in the attic playing trains. I ventured to suggest to them that maybe it was time to come over for the service. Bishop Eric Treacy, of railway fame, looked at me kindly and said, 'Don't worry Margaret, as soon as the 6.24pm train has run and is back in its shed we'll come over.'

On another occasion Michael was very late in coming to church. I knew he was taking a ward service in the hospital, and before that he had wanted to change some light bulbs in church. In his absence I said a prayer with the candidates in the hall, and marched them over to their pews. As the choir, Michael and bishop processed around the church I was horrified to see that Michael had a huge white pad and bandage over one eye. He had the good sense not to keep me in suspense, by explaining in his opening welcome that while changing a light bulb it had shattered in his eye. He had taken the ward service, but sister had been concerned and sent him to casualty, where a metal sliver had been drawn out of his eye by a magnet. Thus reassured, I relaxed. I had every confidence in our new plans of giving the candidates pieces of card on which I had written, again in best calligraphy, their Christian names. The idea was that they held them up as they knelt down to be confirmed and the bishop could then make the confirmation more personal by calling them by name. Always one to save money, and of course, to protect the environment, I had written on the backside of cards from unused advertising material donated by one of our parishioners. It was not until I saw the bishop do a double take when the first candidate knelt down, that I realised the folly of my laudable recycling attempt. Simon, the first candidate was almost confirmed as "KP nuts".

Henceforth I used new sheets of paper, which were placed in each pew, marking the places for the candidates and for their sponsors. Michael had worked out an efficient shunting system whereby the candidates and sponsors backed down the aisle and then appeared before the bishop in the correct batting order. In the early afternoon Michael had been over to church to check my white markers with his master list. Meanwhile I had been over to the church hall to set out tables and chairs, cups and saucers for the 'bun-fight' after the service.

While Michael was down at the hospital taking his ward service, and hopefully not having a spell in casualty, I popped into church to double-check our planning. To my horror the pews were devoid of all my markers. A voice from the darkening north aisle piped up. 'Mrs Walker, the church was in an awful mess. There were papers everywhere, so I've tidied up for you and put them all in the bin.' It was Miss Mandrick of gladioli-cutting fame. She had meant well. I couldn't sound as cross as I felt. Sweetly I said, 'Oh thank you, Miss Mandrick, that was very kind. Now it's still rather cold in church – why don't you go over to the church hall and warm up; it's still an hour to go before the confirmation.' When she was out of sight I found new paper and copied the names from the crumpled remains in the bin, went in search of the master list and soon had everything back in order.

Maybe it was time to put the urn on in the church hall. As I gazed at the empty hall, devoid of tables and chairs and cups and saucers, I knew that it had been a mistake to send Miss Mandrick over there unattended. 'Mrs Walker, the hall was in a terrible mess. I've put everything away and the cups and saucers are back in the cupboard.' Sweetly – but not quite as sweetly as before – I said, 'Thank you, Miss Mandrick. Now why don't you come over to church? It's warm over there now.' I escorted her over and left her in the masterful care of Bertha, our churchwarden, with strict instructions not to let her touch any of the cards on the pews. Meanwhile I dealt out tables, chairs, cups and saucers as fast as an expert card dealer, as I prayed, 'Lord, deliver me from any more confirmation cock-ups.'

There was one more to come, however. It was to be our final confirmation in Halifax, at the beginning of the longest and coldest winter since I had been a hospital almoner in Sheffield in 1963. I had been Michael's organist at the ward service and as we left the warm confines of the hospital we were faced with an intense blizzard, which covered our footmarks within seconds. Battling up the hill to church we wondered how many candidates from outlying villages would get through to the service. More worrying was the fear that the bishop wouldn't get through from Wakefield. As a few candidates arrived and Michael started the service, I was on the phone to the bishop's wife, who assured me her husband and chauffeur had set off in good time and were armed with a spade. I assured her that they had not yet arrived. I then rang the police who were prophets of doom. I gathered that most roads into Halifax were blocked. The chances of seeing the bishop before 7.30pm were minimal. They advised me to go over to church to warn anyone living over a mile away that they should not attempt to drive home, and to put out a request to the congregation for camp beds and blankets in case any had to stay overnight in the church hall.

When I arrived in church, looking like a snowman, I found that Michael was carrying on manfully with a bishop-less confirmation. Hymns had been sung, lessons read, and an impromptu sermon preached. They were now into the Communion, and as I received the chalice I followed my loud "amen" with a sotto voce weather warning and plea for camp beds. This message was subsequently relayed to the congregation which was growing by the minute as snow-bedraggled stragglers stamped snow off their frozen wellies. At this point a tired-looking bishop arrived and began to confirm almost as soon as he had walked up the aisle.

Afterwards, I raided the church hall cupboards for packet soup as an alternative to coffee, and organised beds within the parish for those unable to go straight home. I realised that the bishop and chauffeur would have to stay with us. Their car had been abandoned some two miles away and would by now be an indistinguishable white hump on a side road. The bishop's wife had had the foresight to pack an overnight bag for her husband. The chauffeur wore Michael's tracksuit. We put the bishop in Pauline's room, as it was the only one with a sink. It also faced east. The next morning not only was there no water, but the snow had driven in through the ill-fitting sash windows and frozen into a substantial "snow hedge" on the inside window ledge.

We had the pleasure of the bishop's and chauffeur's company for two nights. As their car was still not dug out, they returned by train. The bishop wrote a sincere thank-you letter and sent us a large turkey in appreciation. It was, like us, still frozen. On the third day just as I was testing its thawing progress, the telephone rang. It was the diocesan vicarage advisor. The bishop had asked him to install central heating in our vicarage as soon as possible. The work was completed by April. We had endured thirteen Pennine winters. The fourteenth was a new experience. We even had to buy a fridge.

The following March we were on the move from the Church of England to the Church in Wales. The first thing I looked for in the new vicarage was the central heating. There was none. The second thing I looked for was the date of the next confirmation. Glory, glory, Alleluia! It was in December and I knew that the bishop's route from St. Asaph to Llangollen was over the bleak Horseshoe Pass. All I had to do now was to rush upstairs. I was in luck. The north-facing sash window was extremely ill-fitting, and that was the guest room!

Chapter 16

We were no strangers to Wales. Michael had spent three very happy years at St. David's College in Lampeter, and we had enjoyed holidays in different parts of Wales every summer, in tents, caravans, cottages, farmhouses, and boats. We had even moored our hired narrow-boat on the canal at Llangollen, little thinking that the gable end in the background of one holiday snap was, in fact, to be our future home.

Was it by chance or by divine plan that on one holiday we had made friends with a farmer and his family who lived near Chirk? The canal ran through their farm, yet they had never travelled on it, so we invited them to travel on our boat into Llangollen. Delyth was very keen for us to learn some Welsh, and so we learned that Llan was a sacred enclosure, that coed was wood, and that pont was a bridge. She made us practise our 'll' sounds by closing our mouths, putting our tongue behind our top front teeth, and blowing out spit from the side of our back teeth. Having achieved a passable grade B in saying 'Llan', we then had to redouble our efforts when it came to saying 'Llangollen'.

By this time we were approaching a lift bridge at Froncysyllte – a challenge both physically and phonetically. First we had to learn that one 'f' was pronounced like a 'v', then we had to roll the 'r', before tackling that ubiquitous 'll'. Then, as we crossed Telford's lofty aqueduct over the River Dee, we were so busy practising our 'Pontcysyllte' that we didn't have time to be frightened by the sheer drop on our left-hand side. We had invited our friends on board to experience the thrill of being on a boat on a near-200-

year-old aqueduct, 120 feet above the valley, yet their main mission seemed to be to enthuse us about the Welsh language.

Three years later we had cause to be eternally grateful to them. The Church Times job advert to which Michael replied, named just three churches - Llangollen, Llantysilio and Trevor. The latter was a doddle, and with spit in our cheeks at the ready we could make a fair stab at the other two. On meeting the wardens for the first time they mentioned another three churches over which the vicar would have care: St. John's Welsh-speaking church, Eglwyseg, and, wait for it, Froncysyllte. We couldn't wait to ring up our farming friends to tell them that Michael was coming to be vicar of all these six churches, whose names we could actually pronounce!

Moving from urban Halifax where Michael had only one church and the hospital chaplaincy, to rural North Wales with six churches, was a challenge. Early on in his ministry in Llangollen he invested in different coloured plastic crates for each church, into which he put, on Saturday evening, all the relevant prayers, sermons, and baptism forms. The crates were then laid in the back of the estate car in chronological order for services at 8am, 9.30am, 11am, 3pm and 6pm. As we disembarked at each church Michael was the crate carrier, while I tagged along as the robe bearer; experience having shown that clergy never appreciated the intricacies of surplice ironing, and seemed incapable of doing anything other than bundling and crushing their vestments, apart from occasionally dragging them in the mud or trapping them in oily car doors.

Each church had its charm. St. Collen's, the parish church, had a grey and rather forbidding exterior completely belying the supremely symmetrical and spacious interior crowned by an intricately carved oak ceiling. Some guide books will tell you, maybe mistakenly, that it originally came from Valle Crucis Abbey, whose lovely ruins were also in our parish. Llantysilio church, where Robert Browning had worshipped when in the area, was set in green meadows above the pretty Horseshoe Falls, birthplace of the Llangollen canal. Eglwyseg cowered below the impressive rocks of the same name, off the road going over the Horseshoe Pass. The weather dictated that at this church, services were Summer Sundays only. Froncysyllte was on the A5, and the journey from there into Llangollen sported a superb view of the Dee valley, over which presided the lofty castle of Dinas Brân. At the other side of the Dee valley was Trevor Chapelry, hidden in woods on a track leading to Trevor Hall. On enquiring how to find it, we were told, 'go up a lane like a dog's hind leg, then turn left up a track, and then stop when you get near the guineafowl. And it's on your left.' The day we went for our foray, the guineafowl had gone on an excursion. Eventually we found this delightful little church, with its dark wooden box pews and intriguing stained-glass window, full of birds and butterflies and flowers, enough to while away the most boring sermon.

Then there was St. John's church, affectionately known as 'Eglwys-y-ddol' – the church in the meadow. Here the worship was entirely in Welsh. This had not featured in the job advert. Initial alarm was short-lived as we heard that there was a Welsh speaking non-stipendiary curate who was happy to minister at this church. However, Michael was the vicar, so he felt he should take part in some services and get to know his Welsh flock. Two things did not come easily to Michael – singing and languages. After 20 years of practice he could make a reasonable stab at singing the versicles around and about the prescribed note of G. But now he would have to contend with singing them in another language! His French master had kindly advised him to drop French before even considering taking it at 'O' level, and would certainly have never foreseen a leap into the Welsh language. Did God have a sense of humour when he called Michael to minister in Wales?

As soon as I could, I started an evening class in Welsh, and found that it was a phonetic language, albeit with extra letters in the alphabet, such as ll, dd, and ff. Thus armed, I was able to write out phonetically, in red ink, the prayers from the evening service. To begin with Michael learned the Grace. '*Gras ein Harglwydd, Iesu Grist ...*' was written as '*Grars ine Har-glue-ith Yessee Greased ...*' This we chanted every night before we went to bed; after three weeks Michael made his debut at St. John's. The small congregation was thrilled that he, a Yorkshireman, should be willing to have a go. Thus encouraged, he decided to tackle the Absolution. Whether it was my phonetics or his Yorkshire accent which caused him to come to grief I will never know, but he ended up by promising the flock eternal food instead of eternal life. However no-one seemed worried by this prospect. *Bywyd* and *Bwyd* can so easily be confused by a nervous non-linguist.

Eventually he mastered the versicles, the blessing, and the set collects. He could also set in motion the creed by saying '*Credaf*' and the Lord's Prayer, '*Ein Tad.*' The lay-people read the lessons and did the intercessions, and of course Michael preached in English. When giving out hymn numbers we found it was acceptable to give them in the form 'Hymn number one, three two' rather than saying (in Welsh, of course) 'Hymn one-hundred-and-thirty-two.' The only snag was that he found difficulty in pronouncing the number six – '*chwech*'. He either sounded like a strangled duck or else someone demanding sex. Hence in our ten years in Llangollen the congregation never sang a hymn with a six in it when Michael was taking the service. There was no problem with the psalms, as the organist had a penchant for Psalm 150, which, apart from its virtue of being short and fairly repetitive, could also be announced as 'the last psalm' – '*y salm olaf.*' For this we could all certainly 'Praise the Lord.'

When we had come over to Llangollen to meet the wardens after hearing the news of Michael's appointment, it was a grey February day with an East wind piercing through the Dee valley. St. Collen's was closed during a massive roof restoration, the vicarage looked drab without any lights, and the town was deserted. By contrast the induction was on a very hot August Saturday with holiday cars and caravans stuck on the A5, and tourists hanging over the ancient bridge gazing at the rapids and at the engines steaming out of Llangollen station. Although it was sometimes exasperating to have to weave in and out of the crowds, or to wait patiently behind a queue in the bread shop while they debated whether to have meringues or chocolate éclairs back in their caravan that night, I did find that living in a tourist area generally made me feel happy. Their holiday spirit rubbed off on me, and made me realise afresh, day after day, what a privilege it was to live in such a beautiful place.

My lot is set in a fair ground – Yea, I have a goodly heritage. Maybe I should teach Michael to announce that psalm as an alternative to number 150. But wait! I must first check and see if it has a number six in it.

Chapter 17

Welsh wasn't the only other language to be heard in Llangollen. The town had a twin. Whereas most towns in Britain are twinned with a similarly sized one overseas, Llangollen was "twinned with the world". Each July the world converged into the valley of the River Dee, to sing, to dance, to play and to build bridges of friendship.

Immediately after the Second World War, when Europe was ravaged and war-torn, there came the idea of an International Eisteddfod to try to heal these scars. A marquee was erected in a field and soon this aspiration started to become a reality. The first German choir to compete came from Lübeck. Apprehension on both sides was great. The singers mounted the stage very unsure of the sort of reception they would get. Meanwhile the stage presenter hovered backstage worried about what he would say in his words of introduction. His brother had been killed on the last day of the war. In a rush of memorable inspiration he came out with the words,' Let us welcome OUR FRIENDS from Germany.' The audience clapped, the choir wept, and there were few dry eyes in the audience.

By the time we came to live in Llangollen there was a well-tried and tested array of Eisteddfod committees overseeing a now vast enterprise, with musicians and dancers from 40 or more countries converging on the town for a colourful and memorable second week of July. By tradition the vicar's wife had been asked to serve on the Hospitality Committee, meeting competitors at Ruabon station, or ferrying them from the Eisteddfod field reception area to homes in the vicinity which had offered beds. I was happy to serve on this committee, and visions of Lady Bountiful serving cucumber sandwiches to Greeks and Turks came rushing to my mind. But this was not to be. I did not drive. Therefore I was of no use. Instead they suggested that I should become a stripper. It was with some relief that, having accepted this offer, I discovered that it was leaves that I would be stripping off stems, as a member of the Floral Committee. I was also asked if I would start by weaving Thuja. I nodded enthusiastically, and rushed back to the vicarage to consult the dictionary. It seemed that this was a form of Cypress – a bit akin to the neighbour's Leylandii which had grown tall and blocked out our light. Pieces of Thuja had to be woven into chicken wire to form the backdrop from which the leaf-stripped flowers would protrude and exude their glory.

The first summer I stripped and wove and filled up plastic tubs with water. I stood in awe at the feet of Jean, Phyllis, Sandy and their retinue of experienced floral artists as they transformed the stage into an organised riot of colour. The second year I was allowed to do two arrangements in baskets for the sides of the main marquee, as I had obviously passed my grade one. I now knew how to boil roses, turn white carnations blue by putting them in a jug of ink, and no longer looked aghast when told to 'go and fetch some Alchemilla Mollis'. My floral zenith was reached in the year the Queen came to open the permanent Eisteddfod Pavilion. In the centre front of the stage there was to be a large three-dimensional crown made of flowers. One of the men made the frame, which was then covered with Oasis to receive the greenery and finally the flower heads to represent the jewels. We had a detailed plan, and I was in my element. I am not very artistic but this was like painting by numbers, and after eight hours of cutting, consulting the plan, and sticking in the flower heads, Gwyneth, my co-worker and I had produced a commendable copy of the Queen's crown. My more florally-adept friends had meanwhile been working on their works of art, which required much more skill. To their credit they did not look too upset when the official photographers arrived and homed in, not on their elegant displays, but on me applying the last carnation head to the Queen's crown. It was a sweet moment in my floral career.

As well as a week of very early risings, to rush to water the flowers each morning, we had a week of late nights. In those days the evening concerts went on until eleven o'clock or later, after which we had to dash back home to welcome our Eisteddfod guests. As the vicarage was only a few houses away from the entrance we had been targeted early on in our tenure to offer hospitality to individual soloists or small groups.

'Where's my shaver?' shouted Michael, one morning. 'Jesus has borrowed it,' I answered, to his amazement. Jesus was one of four Basques competing in a folk instrumental group, and they were our first Eisteddfod guests. Subsequently we had Norwegian girl singers who got through my entire stock of towels, a plain-looking Irish girl whose face became beautiful as she sang *The Holy Child*, a frighteningly military-looking Danish youth who exercised his vocal chords before dawn, and Portuguese dancers who, on leaving the vicarage, gave me a bottle of green liquid which I mistakenly applied to perfume my wrists and neck. I smiled in appreciation; they laughed. It was a liqueur!

Our favourite guests were Audrius, from Lithuania, who looked like a Greek God, and who played his home-made lyre, and Irén, from Budapest, a young lady competing in the folk song solos. They arrived on the Tuesday afternoon, and by that evening they were already part of our Eisteddfod family. On the Wednesday, just before Irén's preliminary test, a button popped off her blouse. Audrius came to the rescue, pinning on to her, with an encouraging kiss, a silver brooch he had made himself.

Back from our duties on the field that day, we were eating our meal with customary Eisteddfod week rapidity, in an effort not to be late for the evening concert, when the doorbell rang with urgency. There stood Irén, tears streaming from her eyes. I was horrified to see her so upset and put my arms around her, fearing the worst. Then, amid the choked sobs she proclaimed, 'I am a *vinner*.' 'I am to sing in the finals on stage tomorrow.' Greatly relieved, I said, 'Oh, Irén, your mother would be so proud.'

Her reply to this, which then had me in tears, was, 'Margaret, today you are my mother.' Michael, Aldreus and I were on the front row next morning to hear Irén sing three short songs her grandmother had once sung on the Hungarian plains, and to clap loudly as she received her prize. She went straight to the publicity tent to buy a sweatshirt for Aldreus, whose silver brooch had saved the day, as well as her modesty. Surely this gesture was an encapsulation of the spirit of the Eisteddfod.

Every year there would be moments like this, which would touch our hearts. One year the Latvian choir was held up in its long journey to Llangollen and arrived too late for any of the competitions. The officials made sure that they were squeezed into the remaining concert so that they would at least have the thrill of appearing on the vast stage. On the Monday, when everyone else had gone home and we would normally have been busy dismantling things in the marquee, we were asked to help in making that day a memorable one for our friends from Northern Europe. A coach was found to take them on a tour of North Wales, and in the evening we hosted a special party for them in a local hostelry. They sang for us and danced in their colourful national costumes, and we soon had them joining in *Oes Gafr Eto?* – a popular Welsh folk song, before introducing them to Bara Brîth and Welsh cakes. They may not have had the privilege of seeing the other 40 or more nations on the Eisteddfod field, but they did share in the Eisteddfod spirit of friendship and goodwill, and we shall never forget them.

For many from Eastern Europe it was their first visit away from their country. When we invited them to sing in Valle Crucis Abbey at the Wednesday open-air service, and in our church on the final Sunday they were amazed at the freedom with which we were able to worship. The leader of one choir asked if we had a bible we could sell to him. The answer was a firm no. We would not sell one bible to him; rather we would raid the Sunday school supply of Good News Bibles and give these, with love, to him and his choir members.

One large choir of children flew in from Russia. They had been given a very small amount of pocket money to last them a week. It emerged that most of them had gone into Wrexham to the charity shops and had used their money to buy clothes to take home for their families. The children sang in our church on the final Sunday, and when the congregation heard about the "charity clothes" they had an impromptu retiring collection, realising £250, which enabled us to give each child £5 to spend. Where could they go to spend it on a Sunday? In the village where they were staying the local shopkeeper broke his Sunday opening rules and let the children buy sweets and stationery which we hope helped them in their long return journey. Their gratitude was out of all proportion to the little we gave them. The translator embraced Michael and me warmly, and insisted on giving us a bottle of wine, and a large box containing twelve matchboxes with fine pictures of Moscow churches on the front. We used them to light the church candles each Sunday, offering up a prayer that there would soon be an end to phrases like "the cold war" and "the iron curtain". Little did we realise how soon our prayers would be answered. Yet 1989 was not to be the end of conflict. In other parts of the world there was mounting unease. Peace does not just happen; it has to be pursued.

The Eisteddfod logo reads *"Byd gwyn fydd byd a gano. Gwaraidd fydd ei gerddi fo"* : 'Blessed is a world that sings. Gentle are its songs.' We in Llangollen were privileged to be part of this world. Surely those whose vision the Eisteddfod was, and those who continue to work so hard to ensure its success year-by-year are worthy of being counted the peacemakers of the Sermon on the Mount. They too will be blessed.

Chapter 18

The International Musical Eisteddfod was not the only festival in Llangollen. The Pavilion, which replaced the ever-problematic marquee, became the venue for many arts and craft events and, with a name forever linked to music, it was not surprising that the town also hosted a prestigious jazz festival. The parish church, well used to the traditional organ and choral singing accompanied by a fine organ, had to adapt each summer to resound to the notes of saxophones and drums and impassioned jazz singers. Not to be outdone, we decided to reinstate a St. Collen's Festival on our patronal saint's day in May.

The different denominations in Llangollen worked well together, with a joint prayer healing group, a bilingual Women's World Day of Prayer, and an annual sponsored canal towpath walk in aid of the Famine in Africa Appeal. On St. Collen's day they came together in the town's parish church to worship and celebrate together and then to process to Plas Newydd, the home of the renowned 'Ladies of Llangollen.' In the gardens we then enjoyed our fellowship over a picnic lunch.

When the assistant bishop was to preach at this service we invited him to the picnic afterwards, promising to have enough food for him and his wife. On the Saturday evening I duly packed my insulated picnic basket with cooked chicken, salads, baps, cakes, dessert and fruit, as I knew I would be rushed in the morning. Unfortunately the basket didn't fit in the fridge, so I put it on the kitchen work surface in a corner which I thought the dog could not reach.

Pinza, our black dog decided that he could. Labradors have an insatiable appetite, and know not when to stop eating. Having deciphered the way to flip over the locking handle, Pinza proceeded to scoff everything except the banana skins. On his way out to the early Communion, Michael discovered the debris-strewn kitchen floor. I gazed at the empty picnic basket, and then stared in vain into a near empty fridge. I felt empathy with the hosts at the wedding of Cana in Galilee, and with the disciples who looked at the hungry crowd of five thousand by the lakeside. I decided I needed a miracle. It did not come in the form of water being turned into wine, or of the crumbs on my kitchen floor turning into ready-made fish sandwiches. It came as a phone call from the bishop.

'I'm awfully sorry to have to tell you that my wife won't be coming with me; she has just heard that one of her relations is seriously ill.' I made suitably sympathetic noises, as he went on to say, 'Of course, I shall be coming to the service, but I really feel I should go straight back home. I am so sorry after all the trouble you have taken to pack up a picnic lunch for us. I do hope someone will be able to have the benefit of it.

Pinza barked; I sank into a chair with relief. The service went splendidly. The rain poured down so lunch had to be in the church hall. Michael and I had never had such a wonderful picnic, for, after hearing the story of the dog's midnight feast, the people of Llangollen shared their food with us – turkey, salmon, pork pie, lemon meringue pie, sponge cake and wine. Then we gathered up the fragments that remained and filled not 12 baskets, but three carrier bags of food which saw us through until Wednesday.

I had not had brilliant luck when entertaining bishops. My first venture had been on Trinity Sunday in my early days as a vicar's wife. Remembering what I had read in a women's magazine about not trying out new recipes when trying to impress, but sticking to simple food, I thought I had come up with a fool-proof menu: tomato soup, salmon salad, and trifle.

After the service I rushed over to the vicarage, opened the tins of soup and put them on to heat. Unfortunately the doorbell rang; it was the bishop's wife and I busied myself showing her the bathroom, and offering her a glass of sherry. As I went to get it I could smell burning. There was a delay in the drink order as I scooped up the remaining soup from the cooker, put it in the pan and added some milk to supplement the volume.

We sipped the burnt soup, and I hoped no one would comment. Then I served out the salmon. I had underestimated how many tins I would need to feed seven of us, so had given the children tuna. This was my second mistake. Pointing to the bishop, Christopher whined, 'Why is his fish pink and mine's grey? I think mine has died.'

I assured him that there were different varieties of salmon, and his must be special. I don't think he was convinced. I am sure the bishop wasn't. I now had to put all my hopes on the trifle.

I had made the trifle the night before, and had been horrified to realise that the big tin at the back of the cupboard did not contain peaches, but pineapple rings - hardly the ideal fruit for the base of a trifle. The shops were shut; pineapple would have to suffice. I chopped it up into small pieces but reserved one whole ring for the decoration to be added once I had put the cream on. I left this pineapple ring on a saucer in the kitchen. Michael came home quite late that night and with his usual post-meeting hunger went straight to the kitchen where he assumed his kind wife had left him a pineapple slice. He had just taken his first bite when I caught him at it, and screamed so loudly that he dropped it in fright. Still uttering oaths of disapproval, I picked it up, rinsed it under the tap and proceeded to cut out the bits bearing his teeth marks. In a moment of inspiration I cut the remaining half circle into three pieces for use the next morning in a triangular design supplemented by glacé cherries.

Following the burnt soup and the dead fish, I brought out the trifle with a flourish. The bishop was impressed. 'How splendid, Margaret. A special Trinity Sunday trifle!' As he pointed to the unsullied three pieces of pineapple he intoned, 'Father, Son and Holy Spirit.' I smiled and nodded in approval, inwardly thanking the Lord yet again for a culinary miracle. Pride was short-lived, however, as Christopher, with a child's unnerving honesty, proclaimed, 'No, that's the bit my dad spat out when my mum screamed.'

I turned my attention to feeding curates, and not bishops. Along life's way we had been blessed with a variety of 'helpers' in the form of lay readers, retired priests, people in training for the ministry and priests wanting to get back into the parochial set-up. None of these curates had been stipendiary. We were therefore excited when the Bishop of St. Asaph offered Michael a full-time one. The offer came, not in the bishop's office, or in Michael's study, but on our little wooden boat on the Llangollen canal. The bishop wished to visit Froncysyllte and, as he had never been on the canal, we offered to ferry him there by boat. He was keen to have a go at steering, and proved to be most adept, and quite oblivious of all the other boaters who stared at the purple shirted man, complete with pectoral cross, and shouted down to their incredulous families, 'Hey, come and look; there's a bishop steering that little boat.'

Just before we approached the Pontcysyllte Aqueduct, the bishop handed the steering over to me, and said, 'Michael, what would you say to having a curate?' His answer was positive, of course. Then it became even more positive when the bishop went on to say, 'a lady curate.' I knew Michael would have visions of a young blonde, and tried to disillusion him later that evening, by pointing out that she might be middle aged and brunette (like me!). Reports of her came filtering through the diocesan grapevine, and phrases like 'militant', 'very strong political views', and 'we think she was involved in Greenham Common', cropped up with alarming frequency.

Jenny was ordained in Llangollen Parish Church having married, in the holidays, a fellow student - a Methodist - from Queen's College, Birmingham. Jenny was young, blonde, and extremely able; we and the parishioners soon became very fond of her. Her earrings were always cause for comment. She had silver ones with crosses on, white ones with doves, and probably a set in each of the four liturgical colours. Always ready to learn, she was also ready to teach. Michael could no longer pray for all mankind. If he did, Jenny would cough, and he would remember to say humankind. When she left the parish she gave me a book of Chopin piano pieces, as a thank you for feeding her on several occasions, and she gave Michael a book on feminist theology!

Academically, Jenny was in the 'A' stream, but she was able to preach in clear and simple terms, and to engage especially with the young people. She also needed to be able to engage with the old and infirm, so she accompanied Michael on his rounds of the old people's homes, where he gave Communion on a regular basis. Some residents were extremely on the ball; sadly others were very confused, as Jenny was soon to discover. During the actual distribution of the Communion Michael went round first with the bread, and Jenny followed with the chalice of wine. When he came to a small lady, hitherto the epitome of sweetness, he put the wafer in her hand, but it was immediately thrown back at him with the words, 'I don't want it – put it up your arse!' Now they hadn't taught Jenny how to deal with that at theological college.

Neither had they told her that she would be expected to be a duchess in the annual parish pantomime, or that her husband would be cast as the wicked demon. They hadn't told me, either, that a vicar's wife who possesses fishnet tights would definitely be expected to be in the chorus line. The panto was produced by Christine, wife of a retired priest. She had written and produced pantomimes all her life, and the thought of filling the Town Hall for four performances each January fired her to yet greater heights. I served my apprenticeship as a Queen in her first production, 'Jack and the Beanstalk.' The following year, in Robinson Crusoe, I had six costume changes, alternating between being a South Sea islander in a grass skirt, a villager in a dirndl skirt, and a traffic warden in a miniscule skirt – hence the tights.

That Christmas I had received a very special present – a folk harp, made in Llanberis. As soon as Christine heard about this she immediately wrote in an extra scene in which Robinson Crusoe had a dream that he was in Wales, and could hear a Welsh folk song to a harp accompaniment, and could see a Welsh folk dance. Both balls were thrown into my court. I had ten days in which to teach six Sunday school children to dance, and ten days in which to find which string played which note, and then to learn *Bugeilio'r gwenith gwyn* sufficiently well to play it on stage. I also had to make a Welsh costume which I could put on over my grass skirt. At that stage I thought being the curate's husband was considerably easier than being the vicar's wife. I had seven costume changes. The devil stayed in black.

The following year I was cast as the goose, in *Mother Goose* and had to wear an inordinately large fluffy and bulky costume, with a beak through which I could just see out. During rehearsals at the end of December I was the only one of the cast who was warm, as the Town Hall heating system had broken down. At the opening performance I was manoeuvred through the wings into my spot by the footlights. Through the opening dialogue I grew hotter and hotter, as the spot turned onto me, and the Town Hall caretaker turned up the newly repaired heating system to full blast. Inside my cocoon of foam and padding I was slowly dissolving into a pool of sweat and feeling rather dizzy as I prepared to do my solo dance to the tune of *Goosey, Goosey Gander.* To make matters worse, as I did my first spin, the goose head dropped forward, with the beak now over my mouth and not over my eyes. Now I was hot, dizzy, blind and completely disoriented. I not only wandered "upstairs and downstairs, and in the lady's chamber", but staggered perilously close to the edge of the stage – to the amusement of the audience, who thought it was all part of the act. Thankfully, the 'prompt' leapt from her seat and escorted me off stage. There I was unzipped and revived with a hand-held fan which blew welcome cold air onto my bosom.

For the next three performances I wore only a bikini under my costume, while the producer ensured that two of my goslings held my hand for the dance sequence.

That goose costume could have earned revenue as a mini-sauna; I emerged pounds lighter, but requested that my next role should involve scantier attire.

My wish was granted – I was to be Dick Whittington's cat. I had no words to learn, but just had to sing and dance and mime. The costume was minimalist – black headdress with furry ears, black leotard with long sleek tail, and of course, black tights. It was my favourite role. Each night I looked out over the lights to see which eminent person was sitting on the front row. This unsuspecting gentleman was soon to have a surprise pussycat on his knee. One night it was John, the churchwarden, who had my tail stroking his face; another night it was Don, an ex-mayor, who received my amorous pawing. To any vicars' wives wanting a hobby I recommend acting. It is so liberating. Try to get a part as an animal; then you can hiss at all those parishioners who have given you grief, and can purr at those who have made vicarage life sweeter.

Hitherto I had been one of the first to take the curtain call in the finale – as a minor queen, or a villager. In Dick Whittington I watched as the rest of the cast came on to fanfares of piano music, and then, holding hands with Alison, the principal boy, I took my bow as the curtains came down, and up, and down again on my final pantomime appearance. My family heaved a sigh of relief as I put away my leotard. They thought it was all over. I knew it was not.

Chapter 19

The size of our vicarages had increased and decreased in direct proportion to the size of our family. The Edwardian Hull vicarage easily accommodated us with a toddler and new baby. Halifax had been the largest house, with its two staircases, cellars, attics, and large rooms making it ideal for the three children in their school years. Llangollen vicarage was a large Victorian semi-detached house with four bedrooms, all of which were occupied for the first weekend there.

Then Christopher left home, the day after Michael's induction, to work for British Rail in Bristol. Pauline did two years at Dinas Brân School, before her five years at Cardiff Medical School, where she qualified as a Doctor in 1990. That same year Rosemary left Llangollen for Swansea to study Environmental Biology.

1993 was a year of change for us all; Christopher moved to Cheshire, Pauline was married, Rosemary (who now wanted to be known as Rosie) started a post-graduate degree in Conservation Biology in Canterbury, and we left Llangollen in the September to serve in a very rural group of parishes near Newtown in mid-Wales. It was an ideal time for a sort out of all our possessions – the Silver Wedding cards we had hoarded, but knew we would never read again, the yellow wallets bulging with film negatives that we might just want to have reprints of, but never did, and exercise books full of laboured essays, quadratic equations and French intransitive verbs. To begin with the process of throwing out was slow, as we laughed at childish spellings, roared at elementary art, and shed a tear at the carefully preserved craft-work given in love for Mothering Sunday. But as removal day grew closer, so did the adrenalin rush of ruthlessness. The presenters of today's "De-clutter Your House" programmes would have been proud of me. I kept Christopher's prize-winning essay on "how to look after your pet", Pauline's hymn written at the age of six, and Rosie's attempt at clay modelling – a monocled pig with a broken left ear.

The rest I put in the bin, though I went downstairs when everyone else was asleep and retrieved my school reports which I knew would bolster my confidence in times of doubt, and would always provide amusement. "Margaret's art is only fair, and her use of paint is poor because she scrubs."

It was time for scrubbing the vicarage floors, and trying to eradicate the scratch marks left on the lounge door by a frustrated Labrador puppy. Time to embark on the parish farewell parties, and leave the Dee and Ceiriog valleys where Michael had served as rural dean. We arrived in Kerry on St. Michael and All Angels' Day. (This Kerry is in Montgomeryshire, though many of our friends thought we were going to Ireland!) The ancient stone church with wide, squat tower crowned in oak welcomed us into the centre of the village, while up the hill the vicarage, a detached white-rendered house built in 1955, commanded a scenic position looking onto the Vale of Kerry. I had never had a 'modern' vicarage before, and although this was the smallest, it had the largest kitchen. It also had a large loft which came with a health warning. It was a haven for flies. Firms had been called in to deal with this menace, holes had been bored, holes had been filled in, fumes had been fumed, but the flies continued to fly. It was a challenge for the new diocesan inspector, Dewi.

Dewi came from St. Asaph down to the southern tip of the diocese during his first week of employment. Michael was out at a meeting, but I knew everything was tidy in the loft. Rucksacks, toys in case we had grandchildren, camping gear and unread theology books nestled under the eaves. Blodwen lived in the loft too. She was the result of a trip to the tip, when Michael had found that a local outfitter's firm was depositing unwanted mannequins. He had scooped up arms, legs, busts, and heads, and spent a happy afternoon trying to fit them together, convinced that a mannequin would come in useful at some parish exhibition. Blodwen was the result. Crowned by a redundant wig which I had worn in pantomime, she was most presentable. Not that I ever saw much of her, as I was too small to heave down the loft ladder, and I didn't know that Michael had hung her by her scarf from a rafter in the corner.

In Michael's absence Dewi had to use the pole with the hook, to release the stairs to go up to the loft on his fly-mission. He had just poked his head up through the hinged flap when I realised I hadn't put on the loft light. As I pressed the switch I heard a frightening rattle of the steps, and an ear-rending 'Oh, my God!' Dewi leant against the steps pallid and shaking. 'There's a woman …'

'It's only Blodwen. She's from the tip…'. I had a lot of explaining to do over a reviving cup of coffee. I hoped that Dewi would dare to come back. He had had a memorable first day, and I dare say he dined out on that story for months. Obviously he bore me no grudge, as he not only ordered new fly-killing apparatus but also sanctioned a brand new cooker and double-glazing. I could have done with him in Halifax!

Kerry Church's priorities, so we were told, were the resurrection of the choir and the Sunday school, and the formation of a Pram Service. It was rewarding work, and we had great cooperation. Michael set out with enthusiasm to visit every homestead in his parishes, undeterred by a home visit early on in our time in Kerry. The local Guides invited him to their fancy dress party. Everyone had to go dressed as someone or something beginning with the letter 'm'. Always fond of alliteration I decided he should go as 'Michael, the Mad Monk,' and set about crocheting him a black woollen fringe to fit around his bald head, to give the effect of a tonsure. Dressed in this, with a cassock, knotted rope belt and with Jesus sandals on his bare feet, he set out in the snow, thinking he knew where to locate the Guides' party. Unfortunately he approached it from the wrong direction, and ended up knocking on the door of an extremely apprehensive lady, who eyed him with terror, and slammed the door as he said, 'Hello, I'm the new vicar. Are the girls here?'

Not only was he the new vicar, but at Llanmerewig he was their new rector. This had not been made clear on his appointment to the group. This church stood on the periphery of the hamlet of Llanmerewig, with many of its congregation drawn from the expanding village of Abermule, with whose famous railway accident of 1921 I was well acquainted, being married to a rail enthusiast. He even had a course of Lent sermons based on famous railway accidents. After his first service there, a lady handed a letter to me, asking if I would give it to the rector. Assuming she meant Bryan, the rector of Newtown I said I would certainly pass it on though I didn't expect to see him for a while. 'Oh, that's all right, she said. No hurry. Just give it to him when you get to bed.' She departed, leaving me bemused and befuddled, until Michael emerged from the vestry, having signed the service register, proclaiming, 'Fancy that, I'm the rector!'

Llanmerewig parishioners were always ready to try new ideas, and the lack of any church hall did not deter them from having a memorable pre-dawn service when they pulled the short straw in a chain of prayer, and adjourning to the treasurer's house for a most companionable full Welsh breakfast. On Harvest Sunday they erected a large tent in the churchyard and proceeded, with flasks, and camping gas burners to produce a three-course meal worthy of the name of 'Harvest Lunch'. On Palm Sunday we awaited with baited breath to see if there would be a donkey to take the children for rides up and down the church path. Jill, the churchwarden, tried to conceal the fact that the sixth Sunday in Lent was approaching, as she was sure that once her daughter's donkey had wind of it, he would play at being lame. Not that it mattered, one year, as we had a packed church anyway, not only to celebrate Palm Sunday but also to celebrate the other churchwarden, Peter, being made High Sheriff of Powys (quite a triumph in Wales, when his surname was English!) He arrived in full regalia, complete with white frilly jabot, black velvet knee-breeches, buckled shoes and sword, and was probably heartily relieved that he didn't have to mount a recalcitrant donkey.

Most Sundays we had to leave the house at 8.15am to drive to our farthest church of Dolfor, possibly one of the highest churches, in terms of altitude, in the Diocese. Depending on the time taken to milk cows, and on negotiating sheep on the narrow road, not to mention snowdrifts, the service started any time between 8.45am. and 9am. Exposed to the winds of the Kerry Hills, and with minimal heating, it was a church which should have had shares in Damart. It was the only church where I needed fingerless gloves when playing the organ. Normally, however, I sat in the congregation. It was here I learned a new local word. 'Why don't you sit here and *cwtsh* up to us?' I was left in no uncertainty as to what this word meant, as I was sandwiched between two homely ladies and thus shielded from some of the draughts.

The Dolfor congregation comprised for the most part, two extended families, who were very faithful attenders.

Mary, the organist, was capable of rushing into church on zero hour, getting changed in a trice, and running up the aisle like a flying angel in blue, in time to play for the procession of the hurriedly dressed choir consisting of her five children and her brother. They tackled anthems ranging from Handel to Rutter, and nowhere have I enjoyed descants more than in this small hilltop, hamlet church on Christmas and Easter mornings.

Michael really enjoyed having more time to do what he felt he was ordained to do. Relieved of the duties of being rural dean, and being part of an innovative 'shared deanery ministry' he could spend more time with people, in their homes and activities, and still have enough energy to be school governor at two schools, on the village hall committee, and initiate new ideas in his three parishes. I became branch leader of the Mothers' Union, joined the WI and enjoyed being part of the Kerry Eisteddfod committee, and having time to make cakes and jam to enter in the Horticultural shows in all three villages.

Our 'honeymoon period' extended far beyond our expectations. The term 'rural idyll' came to mind. Then came changes in the deanery, thick and fast. The curate died suddenly, the rector of Newtown retired, and the new rural dean left to return to academic pursuits. Suddenly Michael was the only stipendiary incumbent in the deanery. Not unexpectedly came the letter from the bishop appointing him, yet again, as rural dean. We had coped with three rural parishes. How would we fare with eleven?

Chapter 20

We had just returned from an 'Explore' adventure holiday in Egypt where we had ridden donkeys to the Valley of the Kings, sailed on feluccas down the Nile, and where Michael had climbed up Mount Sinai to see dawn break. As Moses had been given the commandments on this sacred spot, so Michael came down from the mountain knowing that he too had a mighty task ahead. Suntanned and rejuvenated we came back to Kerry vicarage to work out the service plans for all eleven churches over the busy Advent and Christmas period.

I sat at the computer churning out reams of rotas, forms, reports, and service plans, grimly aware that if vacancies were not filled quickly I would be on my computer chair for long hours in January, preparing for Lent courses and Easter vestry meetings, and again in May doing archdeacon's visitation forms. These dreaded coloured sheets of paper needed statistics of baptisms, confirmations, electoral rolls, population, and how many had attended church on the third Sunday after Trinity. With these we could cope; far more difficult were the annual questions requiring information on what were our parish goals, what three things would we achieve in the next year, and how would we go about making them a reality. At our lowest ebb we considered putting 'Goal number one – early retirement.'

The interaction with people rather than with forms was much more positive. Michael made a point of being in every one of his extra churches at least once a month. We already knew some of their congregations quite well, as we had organised a Deanery pilgrimage to the Holy Land in 1997, and had led a party of 36 around Jerusalem and the Sea of Galilee. From this group emerged incipient worship leaders, lay readers and ordinands, all of whom were a blessing especially in our "wilderness days". Gradually appointments were made and the deanery strode ahead again in good heart and looked forward to the 2000th anniversary of Christ's birthday.

Kerry didn't even have 2,000 inhabitants, but it had a wonderful community spirit, and the people were determined to celebrate. They wanted a millennium project. What should it be and who would lead the committee? Michael had been up the church tower poking around the bell chamber, and had discovered a very ancient clock mechanism, which was subsequently brought down and restored as a museum piece at the west end of the church. Looking at the vast expanse of stone in the wide tower, surmounted by a typical Montgomeryshire wooden steeple, it was obvious that what was needed was a new clock. This was the project and Michael was to chair the Millennium Committee. Enthusiasm and hard work were their watchwords; every organisation in the village contributed towards the £10,000 target. By mid-December 1999 the clock face was erected, and early one evening we had a secret, *sotto voce* preview of its chimes. We awaited its louder official debut to ring in the Third Millennium.

Michael returned from a cold and wet graveside service before Christmas, shivering and sneezing. He managed to conduct all the Christmas services, but flu and bronchitis took hold. In 37 years of ministry he had never missed a service through illness, so I knew how ill he was when he acknowledged, meekly, that he was not going to be fit enough to tackle any of the services over the Millennium weekend.

I had not served on the Millennium Committee; apart from writing a pageant based on the village history, I didn't feel I had done much towards the great celebration. By December 31st I knew that my hour had come. I had spent Christmas in Florence Nightingale mode. Michael grew progressively worse; Pauline and family had stayed briefly and disappeared in a drench of hankies, and Rosie had been admitted to hospital with severe pregnancy sickness. Christopher and I soldiered on; he shopped and went up and down stairs with trays while I made alternative arrangements for seven services, most of which involved me.

The first of my "filling-in" was at the joint service at the chapel, after which almost the whole village joined us, pouring out from the pubs in fancy dress to throng the village square in front of the halogen-lit church tower with its impressive black-and-gold diamond-shaped clock, awaiting the silvery chimes and the striking of midnight.

It was eerie, being on the cusp of a new millennium. Just before Leonard, a retired priest and friend of ours, read Tennyson's *Ring Out Wild Bells*, I had a premonition. What if they didn't ring out? I battled my way urgently to Ray, one of our churchwardens who had received instructions about the new clock, which was radio-controlled from Rugby, and which should have been triggered to strike for the first time at midnight. In an inspired moment I said, 'If, by any chance the clock doesn't strike, could you rush in and pull on the old bell rope twelve times?'

As the minute-hand juddered its way up to twelve there was such a cacophony of hooters, cheering and fireworks that even if the chimes had gone off nobody would have heard them. I had my eyes glued solidly on the clock face. The millennium had dawned and the clock had not struck. Half a long minute later and there was a resounding dong from the belfry. More cheers and congratulations on the wonderful new clock which they thought was chiming twelve. I knew better; I had seen Ray running down the church path. He had obviously learned that a man should always trust a woman's intuition. The next week a new 'chip' was installed and the village resounded to Westminster chimes.

January the first, in the year 2000 dawned bright, clear and mild. The Llanmerewig folk had rung their one bell at midnight, and all our three churches held a short service at mid-day. My job was to play a fanfare on the organ at Kerry. Meanwhile Michael was preparing to make as his Mastermind specialist subject "the worldwide TV coverage of the millennium" as he sat propped up in bed watching a feast of flotillas, festivities and fireworks in between his coughing and snoozing. I missed all this; I had my nose down and pen in hand as I abandoned Michael's half-written millennium sermon and wrote one of my own.

January the second was a Sunday; it seemed to me that we had celebrated at least six Sundays since Michael had fallen ill. My first job was to sing in the choir at Kerry at 10am. The visiting preacher went on at length, so I had to leave before the Communion as I had to be on the organ stool at Llanmerewig for their 11.15am service, then back for lunch before leaving at 1.45pm for Dolfor. I have no idea how I had time to prepare pheasant, followed by raspberry sponge and cream, but that is what is written in my Year 2000 diary. Whether I actually had time to eat any of this delectable lunch is debatable.

Upon the heights of Dolfor the community united for their special service, and it was standing room only for a record attendance of over 150. I had never trained as a lay reader, or a worship leader, and was never in the illustrious list in the diocesan handbook of "those permitted to officiate", but officiate and preach I did on that day. Another duty there was to bless a yew tree, a free handout to any

116

church in the diocese who wanted one. It was an initiative of the naturalist David Bellamy, and the tree had duly been collected from St. Asaph Cathedral, where it had probably had a pre-blessing by someone more holy than I was. I expected it to be at least six feet tall, so was alarmed, just two minutes before the service, when I pushed my way into the vestry in search of said tree, and could see it nowhere. One of the choir then produced a miserable scraggy specimen in a little polythene bag. Obviously its first blessing had been a failure. I did my best when it came to my time to dedicate the piece of God's creation to His Glory. Months later I tried in vain to find any sign of it growing in Dolfor churchyard. It is still a bone of contention whether it died as a result of my inadequate blessing or of Michael's inefficient planting.

I had yet one more duty to perform *in absentia*. It was to help to give out 84 bibles to all the under-16-year-olds of Dolfor. I then momentarily forgot my ailing grandchildren, my pregnant and very sick daughter, and my wheezing husband as I tucked into a hearty tea, secure in the knowledge that my millennium duties had ended.

Well, at least for the moment. I had yet to produce the Kerry pageant in May.

This was a wonderful sunny and memorable day, with a procession through the village, an enactment of the fascinating history of Kerry, with its feuding bishop and archdeacon, Eisteddfod connections, first Welsh Sunday school, its famous breed of sheep and Wales' first sheep sales. This was followed by a fun event on the school field with clowns, and races and band, and finally a ceilidh and hog roast in the village hall.

On such days we felt we could have stayed in our ministry here for many more years. Yet we also felt that much of what we wanted to achieve was being submerged under a barrage of paperwork. It seemed that the new millennium had ridden in on a crest of the wave of public liability. There was a plethora of new legislation – child protection, data protection, and copyright laws. Quite rightly, too, we had to make provision for disabled access, hearing loops in churches and toilet facilities. Many of these requirements needed "faculties". The Latin root of that word suggests that these were to make things "easier". In reality they made things infinitely harder. We suddenly felt old.

Christmas, Lent, Easter, Whitsuntide and Harvest festivals seemed to spin round like a top with ever-increasing momentum. Michael's hearing hadn't recovered fully after the flu, and we were both awaiting operations. The deanery was fully staffed. We had already bought a small cottage at the seaside. It was time to go.

Chapter 21

'Sunrise, sunset, sunrise, sunset, swiftly flow the years; one season following another, laden with happiness and tears.'

I had sung this in *Fiddler on the Roof* in the chorus line of operatic societies in both Halifax and Newtown. Now I found myself humming it as I contemplated the downsizing and packing, with its mixed emotions of looking forward to a new phase in our lives and looking back over the 75 years we had together clocked up in parishes in England and Wales. Being called to a life as a vicar's wife had been a real privilege. Yes, there had been tears, self-centred tears when my efforts or Michael's had been attacked, to my mind unjustifiably, but also tears of compassion at the bedside of a dying person and tears with the parents of the stillborn baby, borne so tenderly by the father, in its tiny coffin.

Far outweighing the tears were the happy memories - spirit-raising services, the fun of children's holiday clubs, the lady who anonymously paid for a joint of meat for the vicarage family each Christmas and Easter, the dance-dramas and musicals and of course, the parties. In all our parishes I had loved organising parties. I didn't go in for dinner parties, as you can imagine, fearing burnt soup, dead fish and pineapple trifle, but I did do parties with games. I loved to see children running madly around collecting different coloured strands of wool and knotting them into lengths. I felt a buzz when a hush descended on the Mothers' Union as they sat in groups working out fiendish clues to my quizzes. I liked to have at least one game where people had to dress in ridiculous garb and everyone could enjoy seeing the churchwardens being mummified in toilet rolls by their wives. I even spent part of my holidays making choir members' names into amusing anagrams, and drawing clues to clergy names - a pair of shoes for the Revd. Walker, a Grecian vase and a beach scene for the Revd. Earnshaw, and a fireside bucket for the Revd. Cole.

I found myself thinking, 'Who will give all the parties when we've gone?' which quote I had always remembered from *Salad Days*. The answer, in that musical, was, 'There won't be any parties.' Of course there would be parties after we left. Parishes need times of celebration and fellowship, and we had often had a new slant on our fellow clergy and our parishioners when they had let their hair down. Conversely it was good for other people to see the clergy and their families in a different light in non-church situations.

On New Year's Eve a youth had said to Christopher, 'your dad's the vicar, isn't he? Good bloke him, really, considering him being a vicar. Done a lot for the community.' That was a well-deserved compliment to be relayed to a flu-ridden father!

Our final social event was a deanery concert, to round off the day when we had held the deanery confirmation. Each parish had been asked to provide seven minutes of entertainment; only the organisers knew in advance what was on offer. The result was a fantastic tapestry of musical, literary and dramatic talent. Llanmerewig church had tap dancers in its congregation. The tap teacher who was giving us tuition for the operatic society's forthcoming production agreed to coach us for our deanery concert slot. The back row of the chorus wore trousers; those willing to expose their legs were in the front row. The curtains opened for the final act of the evening, to reveal Mrs Rural Dean, front centre stage with jaunty hat, waistcoat, and black fishnet tights.

The cucumber sandwiches were there in the midst of a real Montgomeryshire spread at our farewell party following our final service in Kerry when the entire deanery turned out to wish us well. It was with real thankfulness that Michael and I sang:

"Lord, for the years your love has kept and guided,
urged and inspired us, cheered us on our way,
sought us and saved us, pardoned and provided,
*Lord of the years, we bring our thanks today."**

The chapel congregation formed a guard of honour as we entered the village hall for the speeches and presentations. It was an occasion we shall always cherish – a treasured jewel to put in our box of happy memories.

Back at the vicarage more boxes awaited packing. We were worried about weather warnings of impending snow, so decided to stay for our last night with Rosie and Paul, in Newtown. We slept in the loft above the premises, which were soon to open as *Finches*, their new restaurant. I woke early on that cold February morning of 2001.

Everything was different. The bed was different. It had worn its camp bed grooves into my tender hips. Where was my normal soft mattress?

The sounds were different. The toilet made a sinister grinding noise, and not its normal cheerful flush. The light was different. It came from the wrong direction and it was steely grey, the portent of snow. The smell was different – a sickly sweet smell of baby-wipes. I wasn't in my familiar home. I was at my daughter's. I was in transit.

Excitement ruled. I tingled with anticipation like a child on Christmas morning awakening to the feel of a heavy bulging pillowcase on his feet. I turned and whispered

---

* *Text © copyright Timothy Dudley-Smith in Europe (including UK & Ireland) and in all territories not controlled by the Hope Publishing Company, USA. Reproduced by permission.*

'Michael, it's removal day and it's snowing!' Two wonderful things happening on the same day. The prospect of both, and the hopelessness of getting comfortable again propelled me out of the camp bed, to the kitchen for a filling breakfast and into the car.

I sat, semi-crouched, with parts of a model railway layout scraping my right ear, a Border Collie on my feet, two plants on my lap, and wedged in on either side by buckets and plastic bags full of sponges, brushes, oddments of cutlery and old rags full of skirting board dust.

The snow was settling as we climbed the mountain road. We decided to stop on the summit and use our mobile phone to give a weather report to the removal firm who would be almost ready to set off. I looked back to the East – to East Wales where we had lived for over seven years; to North-East Wales, our home for ten years, then over the Pennines to Halifax, York, Hull and East Yorkshire. Running back was the newsreel of my life – 60 years of fast footage: high school, university, hospital, marriage, children, grandchildren, city parishes, town parishes, and rural parishes.

I couldn't look back any more – the snow had covered the rear window. The removal men were apparently not far behind us. We had to get on. Here on the brow of the hill we were on the cusp of our lives. Forward now, in first gear, onto the virgin snow. New tracks to forge.

The dog moved; my left foot was forced into a bucket and the cyclamen fell out of its pot. Soon, surrounded by packing cases, we would be trying to make order out of chaos. My adrenalin romped ahead. I loved removal days!

This one was different. This was to the first home of our own. I would be able to knock nails and hooks into the wall; I could erect shelves where I wanted. I could paint the walls purple. No longer would I be the servant of Captain Committee and Dictator Diary.

We were approaching the causeway known as 'The Cob'. We paid our 5p to get across. I clutched the green ticket – passport to Porthmadog; passport to our new life.

The snow silenced the terrace, as we slid into our little cottage. Winter would soon give way to Spring and rebirth. But right now it was time for a hot cup of tea, corned beef sandwiches and warm, woolly tights.